Broken

But Not In Despair

By

Willi Ray

BROKEN | BUT NOT IN DESPAIR
Copyright 2020 Willi Ray
All Rights Reserved.
Published 2020.

No part of this publication may be reproduced, distributed, or transmitted in any form or by any means, including photocopying, recording, or other electronic or mechanical methods, without the prior written permission of the publisher, except in the case of brief quotations embodied in critical reviews and certain other noncommercial uses permitted by copyright law. For permission requests, write to the publisher, addressed "Attention: Permissions Coordinator," at the address below.

First published by Faith Books & MORE

ISBN 978-1-939761-60-6

Printed in the United States of America

This book is printed on acid-free paper.

Faith Books & MORE
publishing@faithbooksandmore.com
faithbooksandmore.com

Ordering Information:

Quantity sales. Special discounts are available on quantity purchases by corporations, associations, and others. For details, contact the publisher at the address above.

Orders by U.S. trade bookstores and wholesalers. Please contact Ingram Book Company: Tel: (800) 937-8000; Email: orders@ingrambook.com or visit ipage.ingrambook.com.

Dedication

I dedicate this book to my mother, the late great Mary Thomas Dewalt (1939 – 2016). Without my mother, this book would have never been written. She told me to write down my feelings, keep a diary of my pain, and turn my pain into gold. Also, to help the next woman to survive being "Broken" in the fights of life. Her favorite character in this book is Sadie Mae Crenshaw. My mother encouraged me to keep the storyline real and hide nothing because women need to heal each other.

" Momma, I sat on this book for 10 years and now I am ready to share this story with women everywhere."

I dedicate this book to my seven sisters because they are a strong example of support through sisterhood; they never left my side when I was broken.

I dedicate this book to my daughter Janevieair D' Marche' Ray because she is a beautiful strong woman. She has the power to inspire me to search my heart and soul for even more strength than I ever thought I was capable of.

Foreword

Broken, But Not In Despair is about four women dealing with their separate marital issues. Each woman has to battle her own demons in order to validate her self-worth while dealing with a troubled marriage. What will happen when they come together to support and help each other through the support of the sisterhood and female bonding?

Four college friends, who are broken, travel the road to the support of the complicated world of Sisterhood through Female Bonding. I am hoping this book encourages more women to build those support groups and long-term friendships, developed through female bonding because we still need each other.

I wrote this book because women everywhere are fighting to be heard and to exist as equal in workplaces, relationships, and marriages. This requires the kind nutriment and support only found in the support of the sisterhood. The Power of the Sisterhood heals, uplifts and offers anxiety intervention to help women forge a pathway to validating their self-worth. Within the sisterhood, women share their intimate details of love, happiness whether good or bad, hopes and dreams but most of all women feel safe sharing those deep dark secrets women would otherwise take to their graves. Wikipedia says Female Bond is the formation of close personal relationships and patterns of friendship, attachment and cooperation in females. I say Female Bonding are females who are girlfriends and have developed bonds only death can separate. We have a distinctive way of reading emotions and recognizing hidden pain and rise to the occasion to find solutions and protect our girlfriends. We will stand on the line in the midst of a firing squad in the battle for the souls of our girlfriends; this is my definition of Female Bonding and the support of the Sisterhood.

Chapter 1

Lyneil, Sadie Mae, Dydbie, and Benita had not seen one another since college. Now twenty-seven to twenty-eight years old, they were fulfilling a pact made after graduation they would meet in seven years, to reconnect and to celebrate their ten-year friendship, their failures, their successes and their marriages.

Though they had kept in touch, they had not been together since college, and Lyneil looked forward to seeing her three college friends. She walked through the front door of a downtown Atlanta restaurant and approached the maître d.

"I am meeting some friends here. We have a dinner reservation for four for 7:00. The reservation is under Lyneil Gazella."

"Yes, ma'am." The maître d smiled, and with an admiring glance, took in Lyneil's beauty—size four, flat-butted, thin-waisted, big-bosomed body poured into a form-fitting black and bronze dress with matching shoes, gold-bronze-toned skin, jet-black hair cascading down her back like a carpet. Her smile lighting her entire face, posh full lips, straight pearl-white teeth, big round eyes shaded an unusual green. "We have your reservation in the book. Would you like to wait at the patio bar until the others arrive?"

As she walked toward the patio, Lyneil thought about how unlikely it was she would be here reuniting with her three college friends. She was the child of a marriage between a black American soldier who had been stationed in Italy in the 1970s and an Italian nurse. She had been raised in Italy, was bilingual, and had come to the United States as a foreign exchange student. When she became upset, she would habitually launch into rapid-fire Italian, and almost make you forget she was black.

When Lyneil entered, she spotted Sadie Mae sitting at the bar staring at the TV on the wall, which was showing an interview with a Donald Trump supporter. "Lock her up, Lock her up!" shouted Sadie Mae. She laughed and said, to no one in particular, "Wow, America is in an awful place to allow that man to run for president."

Sadie Mae was a shapely size twelve, her pretty cocoa-toned face round with well-defined cheekbones, full lips, and eyes slightly slanted but wide as the sky. Her make-up was flawless, a skill she had learned even before college. She spoke with a high-pitched Chicago accent. Her five-foot-eight-inch frame carried her weight well.

"Hey, Sadie Mae!" Lyneil called as she approached. "To be clear", I barely recognized you.

Sadie Mae looked up and the sun beamed down into her glass of Pepsi. "I'd know that face anywhere. How are you? It's been six years and you still haven't learned my name. Lyneil, you still look great."

The two greeted each other with a hug. Lyneil said, "You look great as well, Sadie Mae. I love the way you are rocking that short haircut. Why did you cut it all off?"

Sadie Mae smiled, and puckered her full, fuchsia-colored lips, but said nothing.

"You made everyone jealous with those thick, wavy curls in college," Lyneil added.

Sadie Mae threw her head back and lifted her face to the early evening sun as if she was waiting for a kiss. "I don't need hair as a security blanket. I love me and who I am; I am not a slave to my hair. I can do more with this cute short hairstyle than with all that hair down my back. Trust, I know who I am and what I need out of life. It has taken me twenty-seven years to understand I am beautiful as I am. Let me know when you get there."

Lyneil sat down on the stool next to Sadie Mae. "I do not disagree you think you are still cute. Why the attitude? How are the boys? I know you are so proud of them."

Sadie Mae smiled with pride. "The boys are great. They are growing like weeds. Mike Jr. is five now, and he is so smart. His teacher wants me to have him tested for the gifted program. My youngest, Keith, is three years old. He is his father's shadow. Every time I come home little Keith meets me at the door, dragging his Teddy and that darn book about the three bears. He loves having me read that story over and over again. I am so blessed to have those two boys."

"Well, blessed woman, how is your husband Michael? Is he still running his music production company? He is a fine man—hmm—but I can think of another word to describe your husband," laughed Lyneil.

Sadie Mae looked at Lyneil. "Be careful! To be clear, that's my man, Lyn. Yes, God has been good to us. Michael enjoys his work. I think if he could, he would eat and breathe his company. It is his pride and joy, girl. I have to get in line with the rest of the world to see him." She checked her watch. "Enough about me, where are Benita and Dyd? They were always late in school."

Lyneil's eyes searched the room for familiar faces. She took out her compact to check her lipstick. "If I know Benita, she will walk in with a cell phone glued to her head and her secretary running behind her with a note pad." They both laughed.

By: Willi Ray

Sadie Mae took a sip of her Pepsi. "Did you see her on television? She looked great and, as usual, she was full of herself." They both laughed again. "She was the defense attorney for some high-profile case." Sadie Mae continued, "When I called to talk to her, she said nothing was as important as her marriage. She loves that man like crazy. I was trying to congratulate her on becoming a partner with her law firm, and all she said was she hoped Raheem was happy about her promotion. She said she did not want to have a fight about it tonight."

"If I remember correctly," Lyneil said, "her husband Raheem is a control freak. He doesn't deserve a woman like her. He is fine though; he looks like a tall version of the singer Prince. His band of medical doctors has been traveling around Europe for three months now, discussing some new medical breakthrough."

Sadie Mae put her finger to her mouth. "Sh! Here she comes."

When Benita walked in, an attractive professional, five-feet-eight-inches tall, well-dressed, fair-skinned, blonde-haired, as expected, she was talking on her cell phone.

Behind her, a five-feet-ten-inch, size four, slender, beautiful honey-brown-skinned woman with long reddish-brown curls entered, her smile radiant, though her glossy hazel eyes held a tinge of sadness. It was Dydbie. She was as beautiful as she had been in college. Her pictures in *Vogue* magazine did no justice to her beauty up-close and personal. Some photographers called her the most beautiful woman in America. She made her way past Benita, who was still talking into her phone.

Benita didn't have to work hard. She liked to appear impressive. Her body posture and phone conversation were dead giveaways. All heads followed the two women as they moved effortlessly through the restaurant to the bar stools where Sadie Mae and Lyneil were sitting.

Dydbie spoke first. "Hi, people. It is so good to see you all after six years. Both of you look great. You will have to tell me your beauty secrets; inquiring minds want to know. Lyneil, in college you were voted 'most likely to become a video vixen.' Are you still doing those booty dances?"

Lyneil rolled her eyes. "Dydbie, only you would walk in with a plan of attack. You missed your calling; you should have been an FBI Agent."

Benita dropped her phone into her purse and hugged the others. "Hi Ladies, it's good to be back with the divas. So, did we get a table? We have so much to talk about. Surprisingly, Sadie Mae, you are still beautiful. The weight—well, you gained a little—but beautiful, yet in all. You have to tell us about motherhood, girl. Before you stop admiring my flawless figure, well, I have to tell you I could not trust this fine cathedral to be destroyed by childbirth. I have been doing the up-keep maintaining this wonderful priceless art of perfection, and girls, I still got it in all the right places. Why are you all so quiet? Don't hate me because I am beautiful."

They all looked at Benita. "Girl, you are tripping," Lyneil said, which made everyone laugh.

"Girl, you are so lucky," Sadie Mae said, "We know you are the opposite of the image you portray." They all laughed. "It is good to see you too, crazy. We don't hate you because you are self-proclaimed beautiful; we hate you because of all the stupid stuff you talked us into in college. We damn near got expelled three times in one year."

Lyneil brushed her hair back and said, "Yes, and sometimes, I still want to beat you down about some things you did to us in college. I cannot believe you sent one of my bras to basketball nerd for Valentine's Day. This boy followed me around asking me out for the rest of the school year. He called me 'Ms. 36C' until we graduated."

Dydbie chuckled. "I am still laughing at how she set my ex-boyfriend up with my sworn enemy, Judy. Judy broke his heart like he did mine."

"And to think I almost lost your friendship," Benita said, "because I was kind enough to help you get even with your cheating boyfriend. I knew Judy would break his heart because she was the college 'ho,' so it was a matter of time before he would find a dark hole to crawl into to lick his wounds." She laughed. "Now can I get a 'thank you,' girl? You know that plan was a masterpiece. His boys talked about him for the rest of the year."

"Yes," said Sadie Mae, "it was funny watching big-booty-Judy cheat on him, and this six-foot-two-inch muscle-bound man running behind her, begging and crying."

Lyneil agreed. "It was pitiful to see. Remember how Dydbie and Judy almost got into a fight? We came to Dydbie's aid, and poor Judy thought Benita was on her side."

Sadie Mae waved her hand in the air and snapped her fingers. "Yes, I remember. Benita told Judy, in front of the entire school, she was not her friend; she set her up with the college male 'ho' because he broke her girlfriend's heart, and those two skanks deserved each other. We were almost expelled from college because of that incident."

"Oh, oh!" Lyneil exclaimed. "The funniest thing was what she did to Sadie Mae. Remember how Benita put an ad in the singles' paper saying, 'College student seeking a rough-neck lover who loves to give a good spanking'?"

Benita chuckled. "Yes, and I had to sleep with one eye open for a month. I thought Sadie Mae was going to kill me. It was an April fool's joke!"

"I did not think it was funny!" Sadie Mae frowned. "You put my name and real phone number in that paper. I had a hundred calls a day. I thought cupid was working overtime, until some guys lined up outside my Law and

By: Willi Ray

Ethics class with a sign saying, 'Hanky-Panky Man.' My teacher called me to the front of the class and asked, 'Why is there a line of young men outside my classroom asking for you and wanting to be spanked? Does your mother know about your extracurricular activity?' He asked me to leave the room because I was a big distraction to the other students who wanted to learn. I had to have campus security escort me back and forth to all my classes. I was going to kill you, Benita, if you had not put a retraction in the paper the next week."

Benita smiled. "I was trying to make you laugh. I had no idea it would nearly get me killed. I love you, girl. Thanks for letting me live."

Sadie Mae returned the smile. "Well, it was not all bad. I met Michael, the cutest boy on campus. He came to my rescue when this one guy who hadn't read the retraction would not leave me alone. Michael kept calling me 'Ms. Spank-It.' I was so surprised, and loved the fact he didn't want to be spanked; he wanted me. It was love at first sight."

"I bet he spanked it the same night," laughed Lyneil.

Dydbie laughed. "Lyneil, stop before Sadie Mae beats you down!" At this all four of them laughed. "College was so much fun," she said, to nods and yeses from the others.

At that moment a waiter approached. "Ladies, your table is ready. As you requested, it is near the bandstand. Please follow me."

They settled into their chairs. Another waiter came bearing a bottle of fine wine and four glasses. As he poured, Lyneil said, "So, Benita, we know your career is going well."

Dydbie picked up her glass. "How about a toast to good friends and great accomplishments?" Four glasses were cheerfully lifted into the air.

After a few glasses of wine, the conversation turned more serious. Sadie Mae said, "Dydbie, tell us about that fine man of yours. How you are balancing your career and your marriage? How much work goes into Congressman Lincoln's wife life of excitement?"

Dydbie breathed a sigh of relief when Lyneil started talking before she had a chance to open her mouth.

"Yes, we need to talk," Lyneil said. "I am successful in everything in my life but my marriage. I work at one of the most impressive Fortune 500 companies in the world. I have broken through the glass ceiling and entered the arena with the white boys. And yes, I am winning. The problem is, for the life of me, I cannot get my marriage back on track. You see, I blindly assumed my husband was supportive of my accomplishments. I told myself repeatedly he loves me, and he will always be there for me because this is our dream."

"What's wrong?" Sadie Mae asked.

"Before, my husband always brought home the biggest paychecks, but now things have changed. I make twice as much money as he makes.

Before, he made all the rules; I did what I was told, like a good little wife. After my career took off, I started making my own decisions. In my eyes, we were the ideal married couple. I loved being his wife and also having my own career, but with all the excitement, I ignored the obvious."

"What is the obvious?" asked Sadie Mae.

Lyneil hung her head. "I came face to face with the fact that my husband was working as hard as I was. I was working on keeping the marriage together, he was working on cheating. His zipper started to slide lower and lower, but it stopped sliding for me. I know his sex drives. We used to be on three days a week, and twice on Sunday; now nothing at all."

"Lyneil, maybe you grew up too fast for him," Sadie Mae suggested. "You went from depending on him for everything to making major decisions at work and at home. You are not the needy little creature he married. You are a strong, educated woman, a VP at a Fortune 500 company, and have the income to prove it. He doesn't know what to do with you. Some men do not want a mature, accomplished woman on their arm. There are men who never outgrow the Barbie syndrome. At what stage in a man's life does he want a real woman with shapely curves and intelligence?"

"I am so sorry to say this," Lyneil agreed, "but he may be afraid and struggling with where he fits into this marriage. His male ego does not want to work hard to entertain an intelligent woman."

Dydbie said, "Most men prefer an empty-headed, short-skirted gold digger. This kind of woman is his so-called 'I made status' symbol. He believes she shows his friends and the world he has arrived. He feels needed by her, and she depends on him for everything."

"Unfortunately," Benita said, "this is a male-driven society, and the rules are made to accommodate the male appetite for lust, sex, and infidelity. Most successful married men also have a younger, blood-sucking bimbo stashed away somewhere. In all fairness, I have to say there are still some men who will never cheat on their wives, and they have learned to grow within their marriages. But your husband is not one of them."

Sadie Mae said, "Most of them cannot satisfy one woman, yet they spend a great deal of time chasing another woman. Think of how quiet bedrooms all across America would be if every married woman stopped faking orgasms."

A hush fell across the table, and then the four erupted with laughter.

Sadie continued, "I want to say, some men cannot take constructive criticism about sex. They get their little feelings hurt and take their goodies and run away crying. Therefore, we women stop demanding better sex and started perform in the bedroom. Some of us should get an Academy Award for

By: Willi Ray

making him think he is the big bang when he is a firecracker." They all laughed.

Dydbie looked at Sadie Mae and shook her head. "You are hard on men, aren't you, girl?"

Benita, still laughing, said, "Don't be alarmed, but if I could patent my fake organism I could make a fortune. *Ah, ah oeoeoeo, Yes, yes, big daddy!*"

"You are so right Benita," Lyneil whispered, "but stop before you scare the waiter!"

Sadie Mae crossed her legs. "Whatever! Can I buy that sound? Does it come on CD or tape? I have not had to make that sound, because as soon as my husband is done, he falls asleep, so I head to the shower."

Lyneil continued in a confidential tone, "I get so tired of my husband telling me, 'If you want sex and intimacy, you need to find yourself a man.' I do not understand why he is in this marriage. Why doesn't he divorce me and move on? He confuses me."

Sadie Mae threw her head back laughing, as if she was caught up in the spirit at church. "Honey…..stop … I am still stuck on the part where he told you—what did you say—he told you to find you a man? Hell, to the naw!"

"Let me finish," said Lyneil. "I am so hurt he can easily say to his wife, 'Go sleep with another man.' He looks me in my face and lies he is not sleeping with another woman."

"Maybe it's another man; down low stuff," Benita snickered.

"Stop it, Benita," Sadie Mae said, suddenly sober. "Lyneil is getting upset. Don't make the man gay now. Lyneil, it sounds like you have been so busy with your career you did not pay attention to the signs that he has been cheating for a long time, and now he feels free to say whatever he wants to you."

Lyneil said, "I was crying one day and my phone rang. It was what I thought was the answer to my prayers. This man on the other end showed up when I needed a man to tell me I am beautiful."

"What are you saying, girl?" Dydbie exclaimed. "Did you—?"

Benita took a deep breath. "Did she what, Dydbie? If she did anything, she had her husband's permission, and that is my legal opinion. Lyneil, you are not alone; there are so many men who cannot handle a powerful woman. Instead of redefining their position within the relationship, some men would rather give up and flee."

Lyneil responded, "All I know is this man took my broken heart and made me feel brand new again. Which had me thinking; men assign women a certain role in society and demand we stay in our places. No matter how educated we become and how we fight to overcome the stereotypical role of the woman in yesterday's marriages, we always seem to fall for the male-domination philosophy. When will women learn? Most men's biggest fear in a relationship is the woman will outgrow the need for him."

They all agreed.

"I cannot help but feel bedazzled by how my man can say, 'I love you' so much easier than 'Baby, I've got your back.' When my husband says he loves me, what is he saying? What he means is, 'Baby, I love you as long as you stay in your place.' Maybe he is saying, 'Baby, I love you as long as you stay the same way you were the day I met you.' Why do so many men feel a professional, accomplished woman has no need for a man?"

Sadie Mae snapped her fingers. "Lyn, stop it; you are upsetting yourself. Can we change the subject?"

"Shut up, Sadie Mae; she needs to talk right now," said Benita.

"Why did he set his mind on finding another woman who makes him feel good about himself?" Lyneil continued. "I will never understand. Why can't he feel good about me, I am only asking for fairness, equal respect, and unconditional love in this marriage? I have trouble believing he cannot love me because I make more money, and I am more educated."

"Girl, I hide my checks," said Sadie Mae. "Only half my money goes into our joint account. You can't be honest with him if he is refusing to be open-minded."

Lyneil dabbed at her eyes with her handkerchief. "I would have given up the world for him if I thought he would truly love me. I do not understand why I have to be stripped down to the equivalent of a dependent child before I am worthy of my man's love. I hurt so bad inside; my heart is broken because he cannot or will not freely give me the love I deserve."

Benita stood up and moved around to Lyneil's chair and reached for her hands. "Please, do not cry anymore. You know I am a lawyer; let me help you."

Lyneil took Benita's hand. "I feel betrayed, bamboozled, wounded, and disappointed because the one man I love more than life itself does not love me at all." She sighed. "You know what is so hard to watch is seeing him destroy with his bare hands what took us seven years to build. His phone rang one day and I answered it. It was another woman. I confronted him, and he said, 'Why are you so concerned now? You were not concerned when you were spending those long nights at the office. If you want sex and romance, I suggest you find yourself a man and walked away.' My soul fell out the bottom of my stomach. I called out to him, and he kept walking and yelled back, 'Do not act like you are surprised!'"

Sadie Mae lifted her shoulders in disbelief. "Wait a minute. Was that before or after he told you, 'If you want sex go sleep with another man.'? Girl, you are better than I am, because it would have taken God to keep me from hurting him badly."

"Afterward," answered Lyneil.

Dydbie said, "Lyn, girl, I do not mean to sound insensitive, but who

By: Willi Ray

does he think he is? Girl, buy you a pair of Astrea vibrating panties, a sexy CD, and a bottle of wine. This is the married woman's savior recipe for non-performing, tired, cheating husbands."

Benita was trying hard to contain her laughter. "Dyds, we do not want to turn her into a drunk and a vibrating panty thrill seeker. She needs a workable solution. Let her finish telling her story."

"Sorry to interrupt," said Sadie Mae, "but in the name of all career women, stop! Dydbie, where can I get a pair of those vibrating panties? Do they come in black?"

"Yes!" Dydbie raised her brows. "They come in black, and red, too. I will not buy the white ones because white is for good girls, and my aim is not to be a good girl. Ladies, I set those panties on fire. Those panties were smoking before I reached an orgasm. By the time my husband got home, I could barely speak. I was still shaking and highly motivated. While my eyes were resetting themselves, I floated over to what looked like my always-tired husband, kissed him on the cheek and asked how his day was. Yes, those panties make for a long, happy marriage."

"Ladies!" exclaimed Benita, "Can we get back to Lyneil?"

"Yes," said Sadie Mae. "He is cheating. Go on with your story."

"We argued, and he claimed his friend who is single and lives alone asked him to put this girl's name and number in his phone so his girlfriend would not see it. What kind of grown man tells a lie that weak and expects to be believed? LOL! It was pitiful! After his brain kicked into gear, he admitted he had a one-night stand. 'An accident,' he said, 'It was not planned.'"

"Not planned? That's what he said?" asked Benita.

Lyneil lifted her head and tilted it up to contain the tears caught in the corners of her eyes. She took a long, deep breath. "Why do men call one-night stands, 'an accident'?"

Dydbie open her purse and pulled out some tissues. "Here, don't mess up that pretty face crying. He is not worth another tear, Lyneil."

Lyneil wiped her eyes and nose, and said again. "I do not understand. How could it be an accident? Did she fall down in a private place where her legs were already open and waiting for him? Did his zipper magically open and he unknowingly had an erection penetrated the woman accidentally? Is saying it was an accident supposed to ease my pain? The last time I checked, men had the ability to reason and make decisions. And he repeated this accident for at least three months. I do not understand men. Why lie? Suppose I told him how I almost fell in love with another man, and how I almost cheated with this man. The things I almost did are exactly what he did do. I am a thinking individual, and I refused to give in to my desires."

"I have to say, God must have had a sense of humor when he put man as the head of the household," said Dydbie.

Sadie Mae spoke up. "God may not be laughing about creating man, but neither is woman!" They all laughed.

"You see?" Benita said. "Out of all the things we build our lives on as women, the man is the most unpredictable and irresistible, crucial part of our lives, yet we build our hopes and dreams on him; we prepare for the future with one of them. It's like building a glass house on an earthquake fault line; eventually it will erupt and crumble."

Dydbie said, "Ladies, unfortunately, God has given us limited choices for husbands. For centuries, women have been battling these life-long odds and some have turned a few frogs into princes. What other choice do we have but to believe love will change their dogmatic behavior, and turn them into faithful mates?"

"Yes, but I am so tired!" Lyneil said. "I am so tired of going through so many changes in this marriage. Sometimes I wish he would leave and never come back. I think I hate him as much as I love him. What I can't stand the most is he lies and cheats without feeling remorse, and the way he talks to me like I am nothing. At one time I thought he was my soul mate. How could I have been so wrong? The most disheartening thing is I don't have a backup plan; this marriage was supposed to last. I prayed and asked God to teach him how to love me, and teach me how to love him. Either God is too busy to answer my prayers, or it is not in the will of God for him to love me. It hurts so bad to keep hoping one day things will get better for us."

"Lyn," said Benita, "I am sorry, but God is never too busy to answer. God gives us free will, and with whatever choices we make there is cause and effect. No one can see the future. We all hope the choices we make today will not destroy all our dreams tomorrow."

"Ladies, I cry myself to sleep some nights," said Lyneil. "*Mi sono pianto per dormire*, because I don't know how to let go. I hurt so badly because, well, have you ever had a man you could not talk to, one who thinks his way is the only way? He does not listen, and he makes you think you are the one who is crazy. He doesn't know how to compromise, and because I have my own mind, I am his enemy. I cannot make him understand I am as important to this marriage as he is. It is so frustrating to know in his eyes I will never be treated as an equal because his pastor told him he is the boss. I wish I had never met him. I am so sorry; all we do is fight. Night and day, we fight. We fight about everything and nothing at all. He doesn't know how to share. All he knows how to do is take and bully. In the six years of this marriage, he has taken my joy, my peace of mind, my love, and all my time."

Benita rubbed Lyneil's shoulders. "Lyn, you are an attractive, educated woman, and maybe you should put yourself first now. Look at your future and

By: Willi Ray

see yourself happy for one minute. Close your eyes. Tell me, what do you see when you picture happiness? Is he there?"

Lyneil closed her eyes, and tears rolled down her face. She shook her head in disbelief. "Okay," she said as she wiped her eyes, "happiness, happiness, hap-pi-ness." She took a deep breath and slowly said, "My friends make me happy, and my job makes me happy. Shopping, vacations. Having a family, a boy and a girl, is part of my plans for the future. But when I picture my future and my happiness, he is not there."

"Benita," Sadie Mae said, "the reason she doesn't see her husband in her future is because of the pain she feels right now. Things will change later. The problem is she is deeply in love with a man who does not love her, and it is hard because anger knows no pain. Yes, it is deep, girl."

Benita replied, "No, her future does not include pain. It is built on hopes, and dreams, and the promises of God. You have to ask yourself, 'What are my dreams and hopes, are they within my control?' Those are the things that are real. So, Lyneil, it is time to move on."

Dydbie stood up, walked three steps, turning her back to everyone. "It is not easy. Suppose he won't let her?"

"He has no control if you leave, right Lyneil?" asked Sadie Mae.

Dydbie's voice held fear. "Isn't it safer for her to stay there? We do not know what is in that man's heart. He may hurt her!"

Benita exclaimed, "No! Dydbie, stop scaring her." She turned to Lyneil. "Do you feel your life is being threatened by this man?"

"He has not hit me," said Lyneil. She paused as a river of memories stayed her tongue.

Dydbie turned back toward the table. "See, she is afraid of him! Why else would she stay in that hell-hole of a marriage?"

Sadie Mae stood, and with her big, glossy, wide eyes filling with tears, said, "Hell, no! Did he put his hands on you? Tell me the truth!"

"Sadie Mae, chill," Benita said. "We can't help her if we lose control. Lyn, when you get ready for a divorce, I will do it for free. I would love to help you get your freedom back."

Sadie Mae laughed. "Be careful. You'd better think about this. She will have you in jail, Lyn."

Benita, in her most authoritative manner, responded, "My degree is in Law, but that was my minor. My major is 'making grown men cry.'"

Shocked, Sadie Mae said, "Marriage is sacred. The Bible says, 'whom God has joined together let no man put asunder.'"

Benita snickered. "Sadie Mae, when was the last time you went to church? I think you misquoted that verse. It said, 'let no man come asunder.' It said nothing about a woman."

Lyneil interrupted, "He lies more than anything else. And he is a coward. He waits until I go to sleep, he pinches me hard. I have awakened five separate times and found bruises on my body. I confronted him several times, and he lied and said he is not a monster; he loves me, and would not do anything to hurt me. Therefore, I started sleeping in another room for two months, but he asked me back into the bedroom, saying he wanted this marriage to work. For two weeks he was Prince Charming, after that back to the evil monster. He lies so much! If this man told me the sun was shining, I would get a flashlight and an umbrella to go outside to look for the sun."

Benita shook her head. "My goodness, is it bad, Lyn?"

"I thought you said he was not putting his hands on you," Sadie Mae said slowly. "To be clear", what are you saying? He abuses you in your sleep, and tells you he loves you? Why in the world are you still in the same bed with that monster? You need to sleep with a metal pipe, and every time you feel a sting, even if it is from a mosquito, wake up swinging. Beat him down then tell him how much you love him. Throw him a kiss on top of the knot you will put on his head!"

"I can't bring myself to leave our bed again," Lyneil said. "I sleep with him because, well, because I am married. My problem is he is a real live Pinocchio."

"You mean Peter Pan, not Pinocchio," Sadie Mae corrected, sarcastically. "He doesn't have a big nose; he is a male fairy who does not live in the real world."

"I wish something else grew," Lyneil said, "but unfortunately only his nose does; it's all over his face."

Dydbie was staring into space as if in a trance. "I know when a woman is being abused, and no one can help?"

"How old is this man?" Benita asked.

"Thirty-seven," Lyneil answered. "Nothing like an old fool! Because of his behavior, and because I cannot believe anything he says, I went to Casenet.com, put in his name, and found out I am his third living wife. The other two marriages ended in divorce because of spousal abuse."

"And you are still in this marriage because—?" Sadie Mae asked. "Steve Harvey's book does not cover this type of man. We must call Steve and ask him if the chapter on the lying male ego is missing or deleted from his book."

Benita laughed, "Sadie Mae, come on! Steve Harvey? Wow! Lyneil, you are an educated, beautiful young woman. What do you need from this man before you can move on?"

Lyneil's eyes poured over the room in the private area. The sun gleaming through the window made the ring on her finger sparkle. She

By: Willi Ray

twisted the ring around and around as she spoke. "I was on my way home in a thunderstorm, and the traffic was bumper to bumper, but all I could do was pray and cry. The feeling surged in my soul during drive was overwhelming. I felt trapped in a worthless marriage. I am in love with a man who makes me nauseous. He does everything he can to hurt me. Some days I pray he will leave me, but he won't. We fight like cats and dogs go weeks without speaking, yet we are married. We are bound together 'until death do us part,' he reminds me, while he is carrying out his master plan of disaster. Some days I wake up and wish I was on the other side of the world. If I died today, even with all I have accomplished, I feel I would die a failure. I would die a failure because I could not make this marriage work, could not stop him from falling out of love with me. My parents have been married forty years. I didn't believe in divorce, until now."

"I hate to interrupt you," said Sadie Mae, "but a divorce is not a bad thing. Jesus said, '...from the beginning it was not so, but Moses made it a law because of the hardness of your hearts.'"

"I came from a single-parent home," Dydbie said. "As soon as my parents were divorced my father vanished into the thin air. He divorced me, my sisters, and my brother along with my mother. My mother has been everything to us. The one thing black people can do, and do well, is survive. We know how to reinvent ourselves, and take things other people throw away, turn them into treasures or delicacies. We are the epitome of the word change. Yes, we know how to make it. My mother sacrificed so I could go to school and get an education. You do not have children by this man, so let it go!"

"I want to let go," Lyneil agreed, "but I don't know how. I have been in this storm so long until I don't know how to break free." She lifted her black hair from her forehead and pushed it back into place.

"I can help you with part," Benita assured her. "I can file the paperwork for you. Please let me help."

Lyneil replied, "Even if I file the papers for a divorce, can I live with the thought I gave up first?"

"Yes, you can!" Dydbie interjected. "We will be here for you. Do not give that man such control over you. Lyneil, it's your life, so let it go. He has done a head job on you. Where is that strong lady I know and love? Stand up! This is not the '60s, when a woman was dependent upon a man financially. You make more money than he does. His male ego is bruised. He has confused being a man with who brings home the most money."

Fresh tears appeared and Lyneil could no longer contain them.

"Lyneil, don't cry; it's okay," Benita comforted her friend. "We know you are hurting." "It's the fact that I have built my entire adult life around him," Lyneil whispered through her tears. "I dreamed of a man who would love me like nothing in this world, a man who craved me like the air he breaths. I wanted him to make me happy for the rest of my life. Don't get me wrong, I know no one can make us happy; it's a choice we make. My desire was to have his babies, but now all I want is to peacefully walk away. I am so tired of fighting and watching all my hopes fall. I want an easy love, easy as the air I breathe, as light as the clouds above. Why is this love so hard?"

Sadie Mae said, "Yes, she is going to be okay now, because she knows the easy love she desires is not in this marriage. We will pray God grants you peace as you go forward to handle your business."

"Lyn," Benita agreed, "you know he will never love you like you desire, so what can I do to help you move on and find closure? You know I have a certain set of fine-tuned skills. Say the word, and I will make him pay."

Lyneil said, "I don't want him killed, but I do want him to feel a great deal of pain and loss. Make him squeal. *Farlo ha doluto cattivo, Farlo ha doluto cattivo.*"

Hire a big thick kick-boxer to beat him down, girl!" Sadie Mae laughed. She added, "Well, maybe not. We are professional ladies; we don't hire people to open a can of whip-butt. To be clear, I am from the South Side of Chicago. Our motto is, 'Neutralize the threat, and ask questions later.' That's who I am; it's in my DNA."

"No, we will not stoop that low," Benita said, "but we will use the law to take his self-respect and make him pay her for the love he willingly withheld from his faithful wife."

"I like the sound of that, Benita," Lyneil said. "Go on; tell me how the law works in my case of a lying, cheating, and disrespectful husband."

"We will sue him," Benita stated.

"For what," Dydbie asked, "a divorce?"

"No," Benita replied, "that will come later. Do you know who he is cheating with?"

"I spoke to her on the phone once, but no, I don't know who she is. Also, I had a strange feeling one day when I went to the mall and this weird woman with short red hair, a big forehead, and a stupid smirk on her face walked up to me and looked me up and down, smiled, and walked away. I was in the grocery store one day not long after and this same strange, weird woman came up to me and said, 'I know your husband. How is he doing these days? You take care.' She turned around and walked off before I could answer her."

Dydbie grunted. "Do tell! What did you all talk about? Make-up tips, recipes? Did you give that crazy woman a piece of your mind?"

"Wait now!" Sadie Mae said. "Now, to be clear, in Chicago that's grounds for a beat-down! You are less than a woman if you let that bold hussy walk up in your face. If you see this woman again, beat the snot out of her!

By: Willi Ray

Make her wish she was dead!"

Benita's mind was all over Lyneil's words. She asked a question she suspected led back to one man. "So how does this woman know how to find you? I suspect your husband is feeding her information about you. You don't know her name, but we can find her by the phone listing of her telephone number. If it is private, I can call a friend in the FBI and have him help us out. I've got a trick for her!"

"I don't want to sue her," Lyneil said, "it's him I want. I don't want to be one of those women who go after the other woman when her man cheats. If he cheats, he must be punished. I did not marry her and promise her I would be faithful until death."

" Him you will have," Benita said flatly. "We will sue for 'Infidelity, Alienation of Affection, and Criminal Conversion.' is the best way to get revenge on a cheating husband."

"What do I have to do?" Lyneil asked.

Dydbie said, "Benita is there a law allows you go after the person whom your spouse is cheating with?"

Benita gave Dydbie a look, but did not answer her. She said to Lyneil, "I will have my office e-mail the paperwork tomorrow and we will make him sing the blues. Whoever this woman is, she'd better run like hell, because we are going to leave some heavy footprints! There are a few states in which this law is still on the books. North Carolina is the one state still considers marriage a legal binding document, so I need to file this case in North Carolina."

Benita stood. "Ladies, excuse me please, I need to make a call." She walked into the lobby and pulled out her cell phone and hit her assistant's number. When she picked up, Benita briefed her on Lyneil's problem, and told her to call a private investigator they had used in the past. "He is needed on this case yesterday. Find this mystery woman's name and address. I want to know how often Mr. Gazella sees her, and where. I want every piece of information he can find on her. Tell the private investigator I want to be briefed every week on this situation until I am satisfied." she rejoined the ladies in the dining room, smiled, and said, "Let the fun begin!"

Chapter 2

"Ladies," Dydbie said, "we need to get ready for the Jazz-fest tonight. I ordered us one more round of peach mango margaritas."

"Good!" Sadie Mae said. "My suite is so beautiful! I can't wait to test out the bed. But I may need alcohol to sleep. I am not used to lonely hotel rooms."

"Speak for yourself!" Dydbie replied. "I love sleeping alone. There is nothing wrong with being away from Big Daddy for a week or two."

Benita looked at Dydbie's sad eyes covered with heavy makeup. "Is everything okay with your husband? I heard he is running for Judge of Circuit Courts."

"Yes, he is," Dydbie smiled, hoping to avoid further questions. "What time is the limo picking us up tonight?"

"Eight o'clock," Lyneil replied.

"I have one question for Benita," she continued. "Are you planning any teenage pranks tonight? Please remember this is not high school. Remember you have a reputation to keep; you are a successful attorney."

Sadie Mae, looking concerned, said, "Please, Benita do not pull any of those tricks from college; we are onto you. We will beat you down all legal-like."

Benita smiled innocently. "Wow! I am a grown woman, and my three friends do not trust me. I am hurt!" She laughed. "I said I would be good."

While she spoke, four handsome men walked over and stood behind each of their chairs. All the women looked behind them, but looked questioningly at Benita.

"Ladies," she announced, "these are your dates for tonight."

After glancing quickly behind her, Sadie Mae whispered to Benita, "To be clear, these are real men. I can't cheat on my husband? I thought this was a girls' weekend."

The gentleman behind Sadie Mae poured her another glass of wine and said, "I am Paul, and I can be whatever you need this weekend." Paul was a medium-built man with a strong bone structure, thick brows, eyes as black as night, teeth bleached white, and skin kissed by the sun. "Would you like to dance, my lady?"

Sadie Mae smiled and asked, "What is this going to cost me? I did not bring much money. I'm not paying for whatever is going on here." But she stood and accepted Paul's hand. "Not that you are not worth every red penny."

"No," Lyneil exclaimed, "she does not want to dance!"

Sadie Mae gave Lyneil a disagreeable look. "I don't want to dance? Okay, ignore my body movement. Yes, I do want to dance. Lyn, stay out of my lane. Deal with your new friend behind your chair."

"Hello! My name is Kendall," said the man stepping to the side. "She is a big girl. She can make up her own mind. I was hoping you would dance with me. I promise I won't bite, even though you are tempting."

Lyneil stood to say something, and Kendall interrupted, "Please don't deny me this pleasure of holding a beautiful woman in my arms, if only for one night." He reached for her hand, and she melted as she looked into the eyes of a man well over six feet tall with big, strong shoulders. He looked like a Greek god.

"You are white," Lyneil said.

Kendall laughed. "Last I checked. If you dance with me, no one will notice I am—" he whispered, "—white."

Lyneil smiled. "I didn't mean it that way; it's I've never danced with a white man before."

Kendall took her hand and said, "Don't worry, I will teach you how to dance on the offbeat." They both laughed.

Dydbie turned to the tall, dark-skinned man standing behind her chair and asked, "What do you want tonight?" He smiled and winked at the same time, and he slowly parted his beautiful, full lips resting under a neat well-groomed mustache.

"My name is Cool Luke, and I am here to serve you in whatever capacity you will allow me. I needed to get out of my room tonight. I am a physician. Benita described you to me, but words cannot do justice to this kind of beauty. I promise not to stare at your perfect face if you give me something else to focus on, like the dance floor."

Dydbie smiled slightly and said, "Well, I hope she told you I am married."

"Yes, she did," Luke said. "I am harmless, and only in town for the weekend for a business meeting. My medical practice is in North Carolina. I did not want to stay in my room all weekend. It is nice to be in the company of a pretty lady. I am not married; my work does not permit much time to socialize. However, I need to relax and unwind. I work so much I don't have time to meet anyone special. Full disclosure, I am lonely, but all I want from you is your company and stimulating conversation."

"I will do my best," Dydbie answered, "but I don't know how stimulating the conversation will be."

"Let's dance, shall we?"

"Yes, I would love to."

By: Willi Ray

Benita turned to the guy standing behind her. "Your name is Allen."

He smiled. "Yes, right. I am he. Tonight, I get to be your date. I won't tell Raheem. "I love watching a powerful woman do her thing. Tonight, I would like to be your student. School me in the fine arts of business, pleasure, entertainment, and balance. Why don't we discuss your views on life and love on the dance floor?"

"Allen," Benita confided, "the biggest problem in my marriage is my husband does not find me attractive anymore. We talk 'at' each other, not 'to' each other. So tonight, I want to feel beautiful in a non-sexual way. Can you color this night beautiful in my eyes?"

"Benita, you are the most beautiful person in this room," Allen answered. "Don't get me wrong; I have never seen four lovelier women, but you are the most stunning. I had to look down to keep from staring at you. I think maybe your husband is working too hard. He may need a vacation, with the two of you. True love is never lost. Sometimes it sits silently while we occupy ourselves with so many other things. All you have to do is find out where you left it."

Benita said, "You are so wise! Let's see what you know about the dance floor!"

The four couples danced to several numbers from the live band. All the ladies had a wonderful time with lots of smiles and giggles.

When they returned to their hotel, they all turned to Benita and said, "Our husbands are going to kill us. This time you caught us off guard."

Lyneil jokingly said, "What would I say to my husband if he came here tonight? I am not a cheater, but I am enjoying myself."

"I am sure he couldn't care less about what you are doing here," Benita said. "Your marriage has been dead for a long time. You need to decide where and when to bury it."

"It may be true for Lyneil," Sadie Mae added, "but I would like to keep my marriage intact."

"Sadie Mae," Benita said, "we are enjoying socializing with the opposite sex. No one is having sex. Relax! I can tell you're having problems with your marriage. You haven't been happy for a long time. This is my gift to you all tonight."

"Benita, stop! Do not analyze my marriage. I am happy; get you some business," said Sadie Mae.

"We will see," smiled Benita.

"Benita, you can be such a witch," said Dydbie. "Why did you have to say that to Sadie Mae? You hurt her feelings. Your marriage is no bed of roses either. You are as miserable as the rest of us; you just know how to hide it better."

Benita paused. "You always knew how to put me in my place, Dydbie. Don't get shot!" They both erupted into laughter. "I am sorry," Benita went on, "You all are my girls, and I care about all of you, but we need to be honest with each other. If I cannot trust you all to love and stand by me during troubled times, why are we friends? You all are my sisters, and I love you, and as far as my marriage goes, yes, I have issues like most successful women. So, ladies, we can all plead the Fifth Amendment when asked about our trip to Atlanta, or we can all stop right now and agree the men need to go."

"No," Lyneil protested. "I have not had a man pay me this much attention in years. Where did they come from? Are any of them married?"

Benita said, "They are all associates of mine. They all owe me favors, and since they were in town and wanted to have some fun—I thought we could help them. None of them are married, but one is recently divorced. Ladies, we are all married and working on our marriages. I have as much to lose as you all do."

"They are all so cute," Sadie Mae squealed. "I feel like I am in college."

In a serious tone, Dydbie said, "Benita, my husband is a Senator, and he would kill me if he knew another man was even looking at me!"

"We've got your back," Benita assured her. "Your husband is always out of town on business, and you travel around the world, so neither of you knows what the other is doing. What he doesn't know won't hurt his pompous ego."

"Be nice, Benita," Lyneil said. "You're mad because he doesn't like you. What is it he calls you? 'Busy-body, power-hungry witch?'"

Benita waved her hand dismissively. "Whatever. You can be sure he doesn't want to meet me in court! Ladies, why don't we go get dressed for the Jazz concert. The gentlemen's limo will arrive at eight. See you all downstairs."

Benita's phone rang, and she walked around the corner to answer it. It was the private investigator. He followed Mr. Gazella to a woman's house on the south side. The detective said he would be sending Benita an overnight packet with pictures and the mystery woman's name and address. "Thank you, Bruce," she said. "Keep up the good work."

Chapter 3

The men rode in a separate limo. The women arrived first and waited in their limo for the men to get out, one at a time. They were all dressed in Georgio Armani cream-colored tuxedos, with gold neckties, French-cuffed shirts, and patent leather shoes accented in gold.

Lyneil said, "Ladies, this is going to be a night to remember, and *caldo e tentare, si' caldo e tentare*. All I can say is, 'Oh my God!' It must be recess in heaven, because four of the finest angels in the universe are here with us."

As the men walked to the ladies' limo people on the sidewalk stopped them, asking if they were famous actors or athletes. They smiled and said no.

"Ladies, it is raining golden hunks of men," Benita announced. "Make a wish while the water is troubled. And keep in mind, what happens in Atlanta stays in Atlanta." Benita had arranged for the men's clothes to be delivered to their rooms earlier along with a barber and a masseuse. She told herself a professional event planner could not have done better."

Dydbie stepped out of the limo, and couldn't believe her eyes. "My husband is going to kill me, but tonight I will die with a smile. Be still my beating heart!"

When a photographer on the sidewalk by the front door of the club came near to take pictures of the couples, the men looked away and the women surrounded and hid Dydbie's face.

Sadie Mae looked at the men with her mouth open. "My goodness, I think I need prayer to stay strong; after all, I am a married woman. Tonight, all I want to feel is excitement and joy. Benita, now I see why you got us all these cream-colored dresses, all different styles, yet dresses fit for queens. Thank you! You have changed from getting us into trouble to getting us to relax and enjoy life."

They coupled up and went into the dinner club. The concert was going well when the waitress brought their dinners. They ate, danced, and talked. Dydbie's cell phone rang.

"Ladies," she said, "I have to get this. It's Senator Anderson. I have to talk to him. He is concerned about me."

"You told him you were okay thirty minutes ago!" Sadie Mae said. "I thought he had a lot of problems to fix for the citizens of your town."

Embarrassed, Dydbie said, "This is the last time I will answer the phone this evening, so excuse me for a minute."

Benita's eyes followed Dydbie's flowing gown down the hall. "Something is wrong with that marriage," she said.

Lyneil remarked, "Did you see how she jumps every time the phone rings?"

"I cannot remember her wearing so much makeup before," Sadie Mae added. "What's going on? We've got to get to the bottom of this!"

"Is there something I can help her with?" Luke asked.

"No," Benita answered, "show her a good time, to take her mind off her husband. Luke, the problem is we are all at crossroads in our marriages, and this weekend some of us will make some powerful decisions which will change our lives forever. We are praying and talking to God, and leaning on each other. So tonight, we celebrate being successful black women, for tomorrow we shall all say good-bye to someone or something."

Dydbie returned to the table. Her face was a new shade of bright red. Her eyes were tearful, yet she smiled and said, "Let us enjoy tonight." Everyone at the table couldn't help but focus on Dydbie face. Her disposition was troubling.

"Are you okay, pretty lady?" Luke asked. "Did something happen with the phone call?"

Dydbie replied, "No, I am okay. Forget about the phone call."

The phone rang again.

Dydbie reached for it, but before she could speak a word into the phone, Benita grabbed it and said, "Hello, Senator Anderson! Dydbie is fine. Did something happen there at home you can't deal with? I am sure you can do without her for three days. You have a good night. I will tell Dydbie you went to bed, and you said goodnight. Sweet dreams, Senator."

Everyone at the table laughed but Dydbie. As Benita hung up the phone, Dydbie was shaking with fear. "Benita, what did you do? Oh, my God! I need a drink." Dydbie rubbed her hands together anxiously.

Luke called the waiter over and ordered a bottle of Spanish red wine. He turned to Dydbie. "Tell me about yourself, "he said. "I saw your pictures in the magazine on the plane. How is the world of modeling?"

"I will tell you after I get my glass of wine," said Dydbie.

Benita leaned over to Dydbie. "I did not mean to get you into trouble," she whispered. "What is going on, girl?"

"Don't worry, Benita; I can handle him," said Dydbie, working hard to force a smile to stay in place. Luke gave her a glass of wine. She drank down the contents without a pause. Everyone's eyes nearly popped out watching this lady who never drinks anything stronger than soda gulp down a glass of wine. This told them there were problems in paradise. "Luke," she said, "why don't we all go for a walk, and I will tell you about my career."

Chapter 4

When they left the club, the couples decided to walk back to the hotel. They talked and flirted with temptation but refused to bite the apple. Instead, they all stayed together and enjoyed the night.

Benita felt a vibration in her pocket and realized she still had Dydbie's phone. "Excuse me a minute," she said to Allen, and went into the bathroom to read Dydbie's text message. It was from her husband. *I hope you remember what happened the last time I could not find you. I will not forget how you ignore and disobey me.*

Infuriated, Benita texted him—*Go to sleep, you're a jealous old fool*—and turned off the phone. That man sounded terrifying. Dydbie was hiding something, and Benita was determined to get to the bottom of it.

After the men left to go to their own rooms, Benita showered and dressed for bed. She jotted down a few notes about what she had seen in Dydbie face tonight. She dialed the front desk and asked for an 8:00 wakeup call.

Benita's head had barely hit the pillow before sleep took over. Her nightmare started again. It was one she dreamed too often. Her eyes moved rapidly in her sleep as she braced for the impact of the emotional ordeal.

It was her sixteenth birthday. The room seemed to rotate around her as fear gripped her. She heard her father talking to her mother.

"The reason I stay out late is because you are getting older, Alice, and I cannot see the beautiful woman I fell in love with. Why don't you do something about those wrinkles and cellulite?"

She heard her mother crying because she could no longer be that twenty-four-year-old beautiful woman he married. As his words echoed off the walls, her mother's tears seemed to hit the floor like bricks. Bam, Bam, Bam. One heavy teardrop after another until the tears filled the room. The beat of her mother's broken heart was like a thunderstorm. It broke the sound barrier.

Struggling to breath in the flood of water, Benita looked in the mirror at a woman aging by the minute. She screamed out when she saw a seventy-year-old woman looking back at her.

"NO! NO! Raheem please don't leave me. I promise, I will stay young forever," she screamed. "Raheem, I need you to promise me you will always love me."

She was suddenly awakened by her own screams.

She heard a pounding on the door. Half engulfed in her dream world, she jumped up, tripping over her robe, and opened the door.

"What wrong?" Dydbie cried. "Is everything okay? I heard screams coming from this room. Was it the TV?"

Taking a breath, irritation replacing panic, she continued, "Benita, why did you disrupt my sleep? Looks like you are fine. Where is my phone? I need to call home!"

"Can't wait until morning?" Benita responded.

Dydbie rubbed her hands together. "No! You don't understand. Please give me my phone and I will leave you alone."

Benita gazed at Dydbie. "I can't believe you woke me up for a cell phone."

"You must have been awake already with all the screaming. I am not a child. You can't take my phone. Woman, please get you some business. I owe you no explanation about why I need my phone right now. I paid for it; it's mine! Fork it over. Now!" yelled Dydbie.

Sadie Mae peeked out her door. Seeing Dydbie and Benita in the hall arguing, she asked, "What is all this fuss about?"

Dydbie turned to face Sadie Mae. "Nothing. Go back to bed, Sadie Mae. I came to get my phone."

"What the hell happened to your eyes?" Sadie Mae exclaimed. "Both of them!"

Lyneil's door opened. "I heard voices and it sounded like my girls fussing in the hall in the middle of the night," she said as she stepped toward the group. "I told myself, 'no, my ladies got class, street women do this kind of stuff.' What is so dog gone important, street women? And whatever it is, why can't it wait four more hours?" She paused. "Wait a minute. Dydbie, what happened to your face?"

Dydbie started to cry. "I need my phone!"

Benita took her by the elbow and pulled her into her room. "Ladies, come in here. We need to talk."

"This is my business," Dydbie yelled, confused and frustrated her secret was out.
"You all need to stay out of this."

She rushed into the bedroom and came back out with Benita's purse. "Where did you put it? Please, give me my phone. You will only make it worse, Benita. You don't understand. Please give me my phone!"

Sadie Mae got between Dydbie and Benita. "I am going to ask you one more time, Dydbie. To be clear, what the hell happened to your face? And why are you acting like a crack head looking to get her next fix? Forget that phone, talk."

"Leave me alone," Dydbie screamed. "I am not a crack head and I need you to mind your own business, Sadie Mae. Sometimes things get out of control and when my husband feels powerless to change things. He is in a position to make change, but because he is a minority, he feels powerless. So, he takes out his frustration on me. Don't worry. Things will get better for us. I got to help him deal with his problems in a hastily manner. I know he loves me and I love him."

"I don't buy it," Lyneil interrupted. "So, you are saying he is not abusive, he beats you because he can't deal with being black in America?" Tears suddenly filled her eyes. "How can he do this to someone he loves?"

"Luke said he felt you were in more trouble than we knew," Benita said. "He told us to give you his card if you needed a friend."

Sadie Mae was still mad as hell. "We need to treat him like he treats her. Let's go beat the crap out of him. I got a crowbar in my car."

"Let's use our heads," Benita told her. "This is a powerful man, and we need to be careful how we deal with him. First, let's talk this through with Dydbie and find out if she wants help. It breaks our heart to see such a pretty face black and blue but maybe Dydbie likes getting her butt kicked on a regular basis."

"Benita, you can be so mean," Lyneil said. "Dydbie, please tell us what happened. How did you get those bruises?"

Dydbie glared at Benita. "Benita, if I didn't know what you meant, I would give you some words to remember."

Benita put her arm around Dydbie. "I was putting it out there. Before I get deeply involved, I need to hear you acknowledge the anger in you, what he has been doing to you is wrong and you are ready to fight."

Dydbie made eye contact with Benita and relaxed a little. She sighed, and said, "The Senator came home and because dinner was late. I was packing for a trip to Japan to shoot the summer fashion wear for this famous designer. I explained the maid was late getting dinner ready because she had a sick child. Without thinking and without blinking an eye, he hit me so hard I flipped backward and hit my head. I was unconscious for about two hours. When I came to myself his doctor was asking me how did I fall and hurt myself."

Dydbie sank onto the bed, crying.

"My husband told the doctor he was trying to attend to my bruises. He claimed I tripped over something, and he found me on the floor. He asked if I was going to be okay. The doctor told him I was lucky nothing was broken and I did not have a concussion. He said I needed to rest the next couple days and I needed to cancel my trip. The men went to my husband's office, laughing and talking about the St. Louis Cardinal's baseball game. My head was pounding and the room was moving. My eyesight was blurred. It felt like my brain was bleeding. It felt like I had been hit by a truck and it was still sitting on top of me. When I was sure the coast was clear, I went to my room and finished packing. I was too weak to drive to the airport but I knew my body could not sustain another beating. When I called a cab, I instructed him to wait two houses down the street and not to blow his horn. I took a bottle of aspirin and only what clothes my hands could carry. Barely able to stand up without wobbling, I found the will to leave a note on the kitchen table and run like hell out the back door and down the alley to get to the cab."

The other women listened in shock.

"I called my friend who is a makeup artist and told him to be on standby because I needed him to patch me up again. Each time I called him,

By: Willi Ray

he threatens to call the police but I always talked him out of it. He is a real friend. He took pictures of my bruises and gave them to me hoping if I saw them I would call the police myself. I have a safe deposit box full of pictures and medical reports, but I am afraid to call.

"I cried all the way to the airport. The cab driver kept asking me if I wanted to go to the police station. I answered him four times within the twenty-five miles to the airport, 'No, keep driving.' One thing I knew was my husband was going to beat me again once I returned home, so I took more and more jobs to stay away from home.

"It was six months before I saw my husband again. Yes, he was still angry. He threatened to kill me before he would let me leave him. After beating me, in the same breath, he cried with me and told me how much he loved me. He always promises never to hit me again. He goes a month sometimes without hitting me. Those are the days when I believe and hope he can change."

Tears flowed from her eyes like a broken faucet and lapped under her chin as she spoke. Her voice shakes and her tone changed into a whispering tremble of fear.

"Please, don't judge me, Benita. I am not crazy. I am over my head in this stuff; I do not know how to break free. Sometimes I feel so worthless, like a penny with a hole in it. Wherever I go he always finds me. He says being a U.S. Senator gives him a license to keep his wife in check. He says he could make me disappear without a trace."

As Dydbie finished her story, Lyneil started pacing, shaking her fingers, and yelling in fast Italian. It looked as if all the blood in her tiny body had rushed to her red face.

"Lyneil, slow down," Benita said. "What are you saying? Speak English! You would think after four years of listening to you speak Italian we would at least understand what you are saying."

Lyneil took a deep breath, sweat visible on her top lip. "The low down, dirty, stupid conundrum of a man." I dare he put his hands on you?"

"Okay, Lyneil," Sadie Mae said. "We get you are upset. Glad we got in English this time. Dydbie, we are here for you. Benita, can you fix this?"

"Che Basso giu' sporca lo sciocco rebus stupid," Lyneil chimed in again, shaking her head. "I thought I had marital problems, but this is unacceptable behavior for a U.S. Senator! We need a plan. Why don't you come and stay with me for a while?" She started ranting in Italian again.

"I don't want to interrupt your life," Dydbie said. "Your house would be surrounded by ten cars of secret service agents as soon as he discovered where I was. You all did not notice the men following us tonight, but they were there."

Benita sat listening and groaning as surges of emotion poured over her like a tidal wave. Her pen aggressively attacked the notepad she was holding hostage. she said, "Downright disrespectful. Why were they following us?" Before Dydbie could answer, she said, "Never mind."

Lyneil's eyes searched Benita's face. "What can we do? They will ruin our trip."

"I love you all too much to put you all through a nightmare of hell dealing with this mad man," Dydbie whined. "He is cruel. He hates Benita, and he is not fond of Sadie Mae either. But he likes Lyneil because she is nice to him."

"We have one person he trusts," Benita said.

"Right," said Sadie Mae, "but to be clear, he is wrong if he thinks I am not nice. He is confusing my South Side of Chicago charm with meanness," she said sarcastically with a giggle. "I am so hurt! Well, Benita, we need a good plan to teach him a lesson and free Dydbie at the same time."

Puckering her pouty pink lips, Benita said, "The first question is, Dydbie, do you want our help?"

Dydbie thought for a few moments, slowly and cautiously, she answered, "Yes, but I will have no place to run. He may kill me before this is over. But I am so sick and tired of being sick and tired of the abuse. If death is the price I must pay to expose and break this kind of abuse, I hope I can help another woman to understand she is not the problem, he is. My husband makes me feel like I should be able to control the beating by not upsetting or making him angry. But I found out no matter how I tried to please him he still hits me to control me.

"I've talked to God about it. I have pleaded and begged for his help. I have cried so much I lost my voice—and my faith. At a low point in my live I

By: Willi Ray

asked God to grant me peace and freedom or grant me death. I was so tired of the broken ribs, bloody noses, broken arms, concussions, black eyes and mental depression.

"While my husband apologized and told me how much he loved me, I could not wrap my mind around how he could say he loved me and treat me so bad. I asked myself, am I crazy or is he crazy? This was not adding up to my ideal of love.

"I never thought I would be one of those helpless creatures who kept a deep dark secret. I always thought if a man mistreats you, leave. Sometimes I did leave, but he always found me and threatened to erase my entire family—my mother, father, my brother and sister. What was I to do? He blew up my brother's car and the police could not find any suspects. That's why I cannot afford to get you all involved. I don't want you to be in trouble or get hurt.

"My husband boasts he is God, and he decides what will happen in my life and my family's lives too. I am afraid every day the sun rises. I live in fear. For me, death would be a vacation.

"We will have to be invisible," Benita said. "All he will see is you. Ladies, hold that thought." Benita reached into her purse and walked toward the door. "I have an important call to make." They all looked at Benita as she closed the door behind her.

Benita called her friend in the FBI. In a low voice, Benita whispered her key phrase—Ride or die—and hung up.

When Benita returned, Lyneil said, "What are we going to do?"

"First, we celebrate our sisterhood," Benita answered, "and we sleep the sleep of victory, for tomorrow we win."

They all huddled around Dydbie and held her and cried. They prayed and asked for God's protection.

Benita heard someone at the door. It was the man from the front desk. He had a large envelope for Benita marked: Urgent—Ride or Die. Benita thanked him and closed the door.

"Who was at the door?" Lyneil asked.

"I had some files sent from the office."

"Can't that wait?" Lyneil complained. "You are on vacation."

"Lyn, can you take care of Dydbie? I will put this away and join you."

Benita went into the bathroom and opened the package. There were pictures of Lyneil's husband with another woman, a young white woman, in a compromising position. There was a detailed report on the woman's life—her name, date of birth, address, job, social security number, financial information. Her name was Cindy Wynhaven, age twenty-three, working at the post office as a mail carrier. Her income was $45,000 a year. She had a new car financed by Lyncil's husband.

"Well, well, well," Benita whispered. "Ms. Cindy blue-eyes Wynhaven, Lyneil did not mention you are white, but your race has no bearing on how I deal with you." Benita took out her cell phone and called her friend to have a warrant for prostitution put into the system, and also to cancel all the woman's charge cards. "I want the new car re-poed," she instructed her friend. "Work on that and call me when it is done."

Benita opened the door and saw Dydbie still crying. She scratched her head, observing her friends from across the room. No one hurts my girls and gets away with it, she thought.

As Benita stood there thinking, Allen called. "I couldn't sleep," he began. "How are you doing?"

He told Benita about a work crisis he was wrestling with. She smiled as she listened. Even though she was married, Allen was a great friend. She trusted him with her dearest secrets, and he seemed to understand her. She will call him again later.

By: Willi Ray

Chapter 5.

Before the night was over, the girls had come up with a workable plan to deal with Dydbie's abusive husband.

At 9:00 Sunday morning, they met the men for breakfast at an outdoor cafe. The gentle breeze lifted the edges of the crisp white table cloths laden with trays of food and thick white napkins. The orange red sun owned the sky. It was so bright; sunglasses were part of their comfortable wardrobe for the day. A variety of breakfast fare and coffee crowned the table. Easy conversation and laughter floated over soft music from the café.

"I'll bet you guys thought we were letting you all go home," laughed Dydbie. "We took a vote, and no one can leave." But after breakfast, the men left for the airport and the women went to church.

As the choir sang, the four friends sat still, a million thoughts going through each of their heads. They prayed for peace and a safe place for Dydbie. They all knew they would be putting their lives on the line in order to save Dydbie's life.

After church, they went to dinner to discuss their plans.

"When is his next television appearance?" Benita asked.

Dydbie looked puzzled. "I'm not sure, but he has a debate with the Republican candidate next week.

"Is that enough time?" Lyneil wondered. "We could lose our reputations and our lives if he finds out we are trying to expose him as the broken-down coward he is."

"We will expose him on television in front of the whole world," Benita assured her.

"How are we going to get him to hit Dydbie on live television?" Sadie Mae asked.

Dydbie cringed. "I cannot do it." She shuddered. "It's bad enough being beat down behind closed doors with the walls to contain my shame. I can't let the nation in on my secret."

"You need to come out of the closet for this to work," Benita cautioned. "I know you don't want everyone all up in your business, so think about it. You got to be sure your marriage is over and you are never going back. Because someone is going to jail when this is all over, and if we fail, the senator might have all of us killed."

Sadie Mae hit the table with her fist. "Why are you all going through so much trouble for this sniveling coward? Give me ten minutes with him in a small soundproof room with a baseball bat and a box of salt—"

"Ouch!" Lyneil laughed. "I hate to ask, but why the box of salt?"

"Because when I bust his butt open with the bat, I am going to pour salt into his wound."

"Sorry, Sadie Mae, we cannot let you at him," Benita giggled, "because you might kill him before we show the world his true colors."

"I am so afraid for all of us," Dydbie moaned. "He will kill us and our bodies will never be found."

"Only if we fail," Benita said, "and we will not fail."

She squeezed Dydbie's hand. "Are you ready to be free? Do you have any idea how it feels to live and love without fear? We cannot live in peace until you are at peace."

Dydbie managed a weak smile. "Let's do this."

"Okay. The first thing we do is going shopping for big fancy hats and beautiful form-fitting, sexy suits fit for revenge-driven divas."

"Don't forget the Gucci sunglasses," Lyneil added. "Senator Anderson hasn't seen us in a while so as long as we are seated in different parts of the auditorium with our wide-brimmed, fancy hats on, we should be good."

"What upsets him most and causes him to hit you?" Benita asked.

"The fact that I am still breathing upsets him," Dydbie responded bitterly. "But if I had to pick one thing it would be talking back to him. He hates for me to disagree with him. He beats blood out of me if I say anything but, 'yes, baby.'"

"Well, the night before the debate, disagree with him, and he will hit you as he usually does."

Benita paused to answer her phone. "Oh, hello, Luke. You have a safe trip. Good. Dydbie? She is okay. Don't worry about her. We will take it from here. Yes, Luke, I will tell her you asked about her. No, we do not need you to come." She looked intently at Dydbie. "Yes, she is a beautiful young lady. Okay. Bye, Luke."

As Benita returned her phone to her purse, Dydbie stood and put her hands on her twenty-three-inch waistline. "Excuse me, Benita, but I try to dodge the butt-kicking, and now you want me to upset him on purpose, so he can kick my butt? All Nawl!"

Lyneil looked around the room to see if anyone was listening. "He might hurt her this time," she whispered.

Benita cleared her throat. "Don't worry, Dydbie. This will be the last time any man will ever hits you again. So, now the morning of the campaign debate he will be so busy we can move without being notice. Dydbie, put makeup over your bruises like you are wearing now. After the debate, when the wives and families come up on the stage, while you are standing there and Senator Anderson makes his last remarks, take a wet towelette from your purse and wipe off the makeup. When the Senator looks behind him to see why you are getting so much attention, while the media is all over you, start crying and say, 'I refuse to cover up these bruises with makeup anymore. My husband deals with his failures in life by beating his wife.'"

Benita paused. "Oh, and before I forget, Dydbie, cancel all your charge cards and move whatever money you can from your joint account into a personal account."

"I am trying to understand," Dydbie said. "Why am I canceling our charge cards?"

"So, he can't post bail fast."

Benita turned to the others. "Sadie Mae, your job is to make friends with the reporters and tell them you have the story of the century. Tell them where to stand and to keep the cameras ready. Lyneil, stay focused because you are to be on point. Your Job is to call 911 thirty minutes before the debate ends and report a man beating his wife. You need to bait him with questions about protection for battered women. I will arrange for a quick getaway car and a safe haven."

She looked at each of the women. "Now remember, ladies it has to look like Dydbie is the only one involved. Dydbie, when he lifts his hand to hit you, like the dog he is, the media will video tape him live. I want you to run and scream. Beg for mercy. The more drama the better. He will chase you because he is a control freak who needs you to be submissive and never defy him in public. The police will intersect him and arrest him. You get in front of the television cameras and tell the world you will not be beaten and kicked anymore. Tell them about the hell you have lived through. I will show up as your attorney and tell the media no more questions at this time.

"Are we all clear on our parts?" asked Benita. "We need to be flawless, invisible, and effective in order to deliver Dydbie from this evil man's hands."

Sadie Mae laughed. "Benita, you are acting like Moses." She sang, "Let my people go!"

Too quickly, the weekend was over and everyone returned home. Dydbie was nervous. She walked into the bedroom and echoes of her screams still lingered in the walls. She wondered how strong those walls had to be to hold in such a mountain of pain and ocean of tears. Regardless how beautifully it was decorated, Dydbie hated this room. It smelled of evil.

She placed her bags on the floor and walked down the hall to get some fresh air. As she moved down the stairs and into the kitchen, she remembered the trouble the painters had covering the stains on the white walls from the blood had erupted from her mouth and nose during a particular beat-down. Her husband had decided to have the entire kitchen painted a brunt tan color.

After that incident, any food served in the kitchen never tasted right. The painful memory lingered in the air of her husband making her mop up her own blood after he snatched her hair and nearly broke her neck jamming ice into her mouth to stop the bleeding.

In the downstairs bathroom, she could still hear her husband's constant reminder to get the mirror replaced. Dydbie left the cracked mirror as it was because she wanted him to be reminded of the night he smashed her face into it twice. She remembered the blood flowing from her head as

By: Willi Ray

she screamed and begged for her life, promising to always answer her phone when he called. That beating resulted in eight stitches over her left eye. Thank God, her friend the makeup artist knew of an urgent care facility that fixed her face and kept her secret. Every time he used that bathroom she wanted him to remember her pain and cracked mirror splattered with her blood. She left the bathroom and slammed the door.

She stopped and sank to the floor. Too ashamed of who she had become.

"Lord, how did I get here," she prayed. "I've made so many foolish decisions in my life and now my friends are putting their lives on the line to rescue me. God, please protect my family and friends. If this goes wrong, he is going to kill us all

Time past and the television debate almost over, Senator Anderson finished his last pitch for votes. The mediator opened the microphone for questions from the floor.

When Lyneil's turn at the mic came, she asked, "Senator, under your administration, what kind of protection would battered and abused women have?"

Senator Anderson cleared his throat. "I propose stiffer penalties for a no-nonsense approach for those who abuse women. Under my administration, women will have better protection and more safe-houses. Vote for me and I will make this a safer place for every citizen. What kind of man beats on a defenseless woman? Women, let me make your world a safer place for you to raise your children."

The crowd applauded and screamed in agreement. The senator lifted both arms in the air to wave at the crowd and to calm them down, so he could finish speaking.

Behind him, Dydbie removed her black Gucci wide-rimmed sunglasses and took a wet towelette from her red Prada purse. With her hands shaking and palms sweating, she slowly wiping the makeup from her face. Suddenly, the television cameras moved from him to her. He choked on his words when he turned and looked at his wife Dydbie's face. She was black and blue. For the first time in years, he felt naked. His secret was out—and he was angry.

Without thinking, he lifted his hand to strike her. He yelled. "You're a high yellow whore, I'll teach you a lesson you will never forget. Dydbie screamed and ran backstage. Senator Anderson truly forgot where he was and chased after her, threatening to kill her.

Following Senator Anderson were Sadie Mae with a reporter, a TV cameraman, and two policemen. She took off her shoes and threw them at the Senator, hitting him in the head, He was so hell-bent on teaching Dydbie a lesson, he never saw them coming, nor did he acknowledge the pain of the impact.

Running after the police, Lyneil shouted, "Please, protect Dydbie." To the reporters, she added, "This is the story of a lifetime! Get in there and get some wonderful shots. Please, don't miss a second of this real-life drama. Ask good questions. Your tax dollars are paying for this wife-abuser to run for public office."

Dydbie stopped and shouted through tears, "I am not running or hiding my bruises anymore. I am telling the world Senator Anderson deals with his failures by beating me. I've been beaten, kicked, choked unconscious, and spat upon every time he came home upset. A couple times I woke up in the hospital under an assumed name with fractured ribs and concussions. I am so tired of playing the good supporting wife. This man should be running a campaign in hell. I cannot tell the world the nightmare I have been living. I need peace. America, this is your United States Senator. Do not vote for him!"

When Sadie Mae caught up to her friend she screamed, "Hit her again, and I will beat you down, clown!"

She was about to throw a bottle of water at Senator Anderson when a tall man stepped in front of her, took the bottle from her hands and said, "Let me handle this one, pretty lady."

Senator Anderson took a swing at Dydbie. She ducked, and Luke punched him in the nose. He dropped like a rock, unconscious.

Benita had joined the group of people staring down at the political figure on the floor. She looked at Luke. "Where did you come from? I hope this won't become an obstacle during the divorce. Whoa! One punch, Luke. I need to get you out of camera range before the reporters ask questions. The last thing we need is a scandal of infidelity."

Dydbie turned to Luke, shock on her face. "What are you doing here?"

By: Willi Ray

"I felt like you could use a little extra help," Luke answered.

Benita caught Lyneil's arm. "Quick! Do something to take the heat off Luke."

"I thought we were supposed to keep a low profile," Lyneil responded.

"Do it!" Benita whispered through her teeth.

"Okay, if you say so!" Lyneil pushed into the center of the confusion and fainted. All the attention turned to her.

Benita grabbed Luke. "Get out of here! Now!"

"Why?" asked Luke.

"I will explain later. Keep your head down and walk away."

Benita breathed a sigh of relief as Luke faded into the crowd of onlookers.

Sadie Mae stepped to the edge of the crowd. "Is there a doctor in the house? Please call an ambulance when you are done arresting Senator Anderson." She bent over and whispered to Lyneil, "Luke is gone. Get up."

Lyneil's eyes fluttered open, and she lifted her head, looking around the room as if in a daze. "I am sorry. With all the confusion, I got so light-headed. Please excuse me; I did not mean to alarm everyone. I will have myself checked out."

The police put some smelling salts under the Senator's nose and got him to his feet. They handcuffed him.

"Dydbie, tell them I never touched you," he yelled at his wife. "This is all a mistake. Please, Dydbie, don't let them take me to jail."

He tried to pull away from the policeman holding his arms. "My wife will not press charges," he sneered over his shoulder to the one behind him. "I will have all of you fired. I will have your jobs, you kindergarten cops. Do you know who I am? I run this town."

Trying to resist the policemen moving him away, he called to Dydbie, "Baby, come over here and tell them this is a great big misunderstanding."

"I plan to tell them all about it," Dydbie said calmly. "Don't you worry. I got this. I am going to make sure you get everything coming to you. Starting with this." She kneed him in his crotch.

He dropped to his knees in pain.

"Your butt-kicking skills will get plenty of exercise in jail when you have to fight every night to keep big Bubba off your butt," she continued. "Good luck with that!"

The Senator bent forward in pain until the policemen pulled him to his feet.

A reporter pushed a microphone toward Dydbie. "Mrs. Anderson, why didn't you report this to the police?"

"I did," she answered.

A second reporter asked, "Was your husband ever arrested?"

"No," Dydbie responded. "He is not a man without influence. He has most of the police department on a short leash."

"How did you survive five years of marriage with this kind of abuse?" the first reporter asked.

"By the grace of God and the help of my friends," she said.

Benita stepped between Dydbie and the reporters. "Mrs. Anderson is my client. Therefore, she is answering no more questions at this time. This was an unfortunate incident today. My client is in desperate need of medical attention and legal counsel."

Dydbie put on her wide-brimmed yellow hat with her Gucci sunglasses. As the police led Senator Anderson toward the squad car, three well-dressed ladies in wide-brimmed dressy hats and gloves to match—purple, pink, and orange—watched as he passed.

Lyneil stuck out one leg and tripped the Senator.

"I am so sorry," she said sweetly. "I was fixing my shoe. Pops!"

Senator Anderson fell on his face.

By: Willi Ray

As he looked up from the ground, the ladies removed their hats, smiled, and winked at him. They turned and walked away.

"I'll get the four of you," the Senator said under his breath. "You all will be so sorry."

Benita escorted her client away from the scene. "Dydbie, you are coming home with me," she said. "I want to make sure you are safe."

"No, I have servants who will take care of me," Dydbie responded. "I feel free, like waking up from a bad dream. It feels so good to know I will never be hit again. No man will raise his hands to me ever again. Well, wait," she laughed. "Not unless it's a love spanking."

Sadie Mae said, "You little freak! That's what got you into this situation."

"Leave the girl alone," said Lyneil folding her arms under her breasts. "She knows if she wants to be spanked or not."

"I will pack a few things and be in New York by morning," Dydbie concluded.

Still excited by their success, Sadie Mae gloated, "We bad! We are some bad Mama Jama! Please go home and pack so Benita can protect you. You know as soon as Senator Anderson can make his one phone call, he will call his goons."

Lyneil laughed "Yeah, Sadie Mae, we used girl power to take him down. Benita, your plan was perfect. What you say your degree was in again? To quote you, 'Making grown men weep bitter tears?'"

Benita clapped her hands and said, "The man had no idea his career, his marriage, and his life as he knew it were over. It will be my pleasure to make sure he regrets the day he was born."

Chapter 6

While Dydbie packed her bags, the doorbell rang. "Please get the door," she called down to the servants from her bedroom.

The bell sounded again.

"Where is everyone?" she asked herself. She called again, "Sam, you're the butler. Get the door."

The bell sounded a third time.

Dydbie quickly bounced down the stairs and went into the kitchen. Where could the maid be? "Na'dada, are you here?"

She went through all the downstairs rooms. In the fifteen-room mansion, she could not find any of the servants. All of a sudden, her deepest fear stared her in the face. The house felt big and frightening. Sweat and panic were visual signs. Dydbie was now in the Twilight Zone. Nothing was as it appeared.

Slowly, she approached the door. Through the stained-glass window, she saw the form of a full-figured man wearing a hat. She blinked. "Who's there?" she called, trying to steady the tremor in her voice.

No answer.

Gripping the mace on her keychain, she opened the door. No one was there—a note. She looked around and saw no one. She opened the note. *A husband has the rights to discipline his disobedient wife.*

Shaking, she slammed the door and went back to her bedroom to resume her packing.

As soon as she was back upstairs, the doorbell rang again. She heard the patter of shoes on the hardwood floors below. Every step made her heart pound. She got into the closet and covered her mouth to stifle the sound of her whimpers. Her knees were knocking so hard they started to hurt and burned. She was sure the drumbeat of her heart would give her way. She heard her bedroom door open as if in a scary horror movie. Grabbing a golf club beside her, she squeezed to the back of the closet. The door knob giggled and rattled, the door opened. Dydbie jumped out, swinging the golf club and screaming.

Quick thinking Benita blocked the golf club in mid-air and snatched it from Dydbie's hand.

Dydbie fell into Benita's arms, crying hysterically. "Someone was ringing the doorbell and wouldn't stop," she sobbed.

Benita looking puzzled. "I thought you could use a ride to the airport. I didn't see anyone when my limo drove up. Where are the servants?"

"I was so afraid," Dydbie continued. "I called for Sam and Na'dada but no one answered. I know he is going to kill me. I know it."

Benita held her friend and let her cry. "Go ahead, get it out. We are here to protect you." When Dydbie stopped shaking, Benita said, "Come on. We need to find out what happened to the servants."

Benita made a phone call. "Na'dada, this is Mrs. Anderson's attorney, Benita Porter. Were you supposed to work at the Anderson house tonight?"

"A man came by when I was getting ready to make dinner," Na'dada said. "He said Sam and I would not be needed this week, and we were to take the week off with pay. Do you need me to come back?"

"Have you ever seen this man before?"

"No. He was fat, a middle-aged white man with a beard. He seemed kind and gentle."

"Thank you, Na'dada."

After Benita hung up, Dydbie showed her the note that had been left earlier.

"I found a second note on the floor when I came in," Benita told her.

"What did it say?" Dydbie trembled again.

Benita stuck the scrummed-up piece of paper with a typed message into her pocket. "Nothing you need to know right now. We will discuss it later.

By: Willi Ray

I will take care of this for you, Dydbie. Let's get you out of town."

"Where are the other girls?"

"They are on their way to the airport. They said they will call you tomorrow."

"When will I ever be able to stop looking over my shoulders? Is there peace after Senator Anderson?"

"Dydbie, today is the last day you will cry because you are afraid. I promise."

Benita helped Dydbie gather her things. Before she climbed into the limo Dydbie looked one last time at the neat white mansion with the manicured lawns and poinsettias on the porch, the tall French wrought iron fence and cobblestone walkway.

"Come on, girl," Benita said gently. "No use reminiscing over the unhappy marriage you had in this beautiful hell-hole. We need to get you checked for CTE because of all the beatings and concussions you suffered."

Dydbie sank into the limo and cried again. "I am so glad it is over."

A few minutes into the trip to the airport, she calmed again. "What is CTE?" she asked. "Isn't that a sports injury?"

Benita explained Chronic Traumatic Encephalopathy is caused by concussion and repeated head injury and can affect memory, mood, and behavior.

"I want to make sure you are okay," she said. "Some abused women who stay much too long in those relationships, being battered night and day, suffer from CTE. If athletes, who are a lot stronger than women, develops this disease from repeated concussions, why do people not understand battered women should be tested for this as well?"

As the limo wound through traffic, Dydbie stared out the window. "Now that I am free from the butt kicking, I have to worry about CTE. When I was thinking nightmares and shell shock were my biggest problems. Wow! Life has no mercy."

Benita squeezed Dydbie's hand. "We will make an appointment when you are dead! The only way to truly test for this is when you are dead." They both laughed.

"I am going to live," Dydbie shouted.

At home in New York, Benita called to her secretary, "Get me the commissioner of state prisons. I need a favor," she said. "I need to arrange for a beat down of an inmate, Senator Anderson. I don't want him killed or severely disfigured. I want him to be sore, kind of like black and blue. Make it a black eye and a cherry on top. Beat him like a rented mule remind him every time he messes with Dydbie this process will be repeated."

The night in the jail, as the guard called out the code to lock down the units and cells, Senator Anderson happened to meet big Bubba, a walking nightmare, who hit like Mike Tyson. He screamed out for help but no one came to his rescue. He thought ten men jumped him that night. All he saw was one fast flying fat fist after another. He laid there in his own blood, bruised from head to toe. He slept in his own blood that night because he could not move. The last thing he heard before losing consciousness was, "Never ever mess with Dydbie Anderson, or we will repeat this process every night."

Benita received a call from the jail. A low voice said, "It is done."

"I need proof he understands never to think about hurting Dydbie or her family ever again. Send me the big toe on his right foot by the end of the week as proof." She took out her checkbook, wrote thank you on a card, and put it all in an envelope. She called for room service to mail it ASAP.

Benita called her friend that night. "Dydbie, you made the news."

"I know," she answered. "I heard from my modeling agency. They are concerned this may change my image. They are waiting for the fallout before starting damage control. I may never work in this industry again. I have a fashion line and a makeup line that could take a nose dive."

Dydbie flopped onto the bed and covered her face with her hands. "Bea, I am so tired. I have hidden my family in another state where I am hoping he can't find them. I am relieved and stressed all at the same time. But one thing is for sure. I am glad not to be worried about getting beat down tonight. Call me tomorrow please. I am tired now."

By: Willi Ray

"Do you want to keep modeling and save your company's reputation? I can put a positive spin on all this."

"Yes, of course."

"Let me make a few phone calls."

Benita called a violence-against-women organization and offered them an exclusive story and a model spokesperson for fundraising and to help get their message out. She called all the major television networks to set up interviews. She called Oprah Winfrey to book an interview to discuss a positive spin on the battered wife of a senator who took steps to make sure all abused women have a voice and to bring awareness to battered women syndrome.

When Benita got up early the next morning to make some coffee, steam was pouring from the crack under the bathroom door. This was evidence her husband Raheem was home and getting ready for work. He came out of the bathroom wearing a towel around his waist, steam surrounding his body like smoke. He kissed his wife on the cheek.

Benita looked at her handsome husband. "Let me guess," she said, "no time for breakfast? Early morning meeting?"

Raheem stopped and stared at her. "Honey, this in important now. Be patient."

His freshly-shaven face touched her cheek. In a few minutes, he was dressed and out the door.

Her phone rang. It was Raheem.

"Honey, there is a UPS package on the table for you. Have a good day." Before she could answer, he hung up.

Benita opened the box. It was a man's severed big toe. Oh, my, Benita thought. What a nasty sight. She wrapped the box in plastic and put it in the trash. Good thing the trash man was coming today. She called for her maid to get ready for the day.

Chapter 7

Months passed uneventfully. One day, Benita got a call from Sadie Mae.

"How is Chicago this time of the year?" Benita asked.

Sadie Mae ignored the chit chat. "I am so mad with my husband," she said. "We have been at odds for three months."

Benita stopped what she was doing. "So, Chicago is not so good right now? Sadie Mae, it's only been three months since your weekend away. Wasn't he glad to see you when you got home?"

"No, all he said was, 'You are looking bigger than you did when you left.'"

Benita pulled the chair out from her desk and sat down. "Hold on, Sadie Mae. I need to call the ladies. You need all the support you can get."

She dialed the numbers and conference in the other two friends.

"Hey ladies," Benita began. "Sadie Mae is on the phone, and she needs us to help her work through some marital problems. I have four days free next month. Why don't we meet in Montego Bay, Jamaica?"

"I have a meeting with an important client next week," Lyneil responded, "but I will reschedule it for an earlier date. I am here for my girls. I look forward to our time together."

"I can make it," Dydbie said. "But I have a new ad campaign coming up in three weeks. Sadie Mae, hold on. We love you."

"Great. Ladies, see you all in Jamaica."

"Benita, please don't get any ideas about the nude beaches," Lyneil teased.

Sadie Mae groaned. "Please tell me the beach where we will be staying is not a nude beach."

"I won't tell you."

"Nude is a natural state," Dydbie chimed in. "I love my body, and I also like sightseeing. I hope the men have a volleyball game going when we get there."

Dydbie got another call. "Wait a minute," she said. "This is Oprah Winfrey to discuss my interview about battered women in bad marriages.

"Dydbie knows how to relax," Benita said. "Some things are out of our control. I love seeing a muscle-bound man leap into the air to hit a ball."

"OMG!" Dydbie screamed when she came back to their call. "I got the interview with Oprah Winfrey scheduled."

"Really? That is wonderful," Lyneil said. "Was Oprah on the phone or her business and production manager?"

"Wow! I have nothing to wear to be on TV," Sadie Mae complained. "I need to get my hair done. When do we go?"

"Next Friday," Dydbie said.

"I am sorry, but is not enough time. I got to get beautiful."

"I am sorry, Sadie Mae, but this is not about you," Lyneil said. "This is about Dydbie."

"Right Lyn," Sadie Mae laughed. "Now, shut up. Dydbie is my best friend. She and I will tell Oprah the whole story."

Benita laughed. "This is God turning Dydbie's pain into a pot of gold. Don't block her blessing."

"Okay, you all are right," Sadie Mae admitted. "Dydbie, if you need us we are here. I will give you the spotlight though."

"Tell your story," Lyneil said. "Lord knows you earned it."

"Benita, I know you got something up your sleeve. We are at your mercy," Sadie Mae said. "Lyneil, what did you do about your husband?"

"I am taking him to court," Lyneil replied. "I am suing him for breach of contract. Yes, it is true there are seven states in which cheaters should

By: Willi Ray

beware: Mississippi, Hawaii, Illinois, New Mexico, North Carolina, and Utah. So, since I don't happen to live in any of those states, I bought a condo in Hawaii and I have been going there one weekend a month for the last three months."

"Hmm—" Sadie Mae said, "—I know your Italian roots run deep, but you cannot sue a man for cheating on you. We thought you two were kidding about suing your cheating husband.

"No girl," Dydbie laughed, "you are not suing him for infidelity. Whoa!"

Benita responded in her lawyer voice, "There is no law that she cannot sue him. We will keep you all posted on how to sue your husband's for cheating. We are using the law to correct the male DNA."

At the airport in Jamaica, when all the friends had gotten off their planes, they found a cab. With only one bag each, they headed for the resort in Montego Bay.

"It is so beautiful here," Benita said.

Sadie Mae agreed. "This is my first time in Jamaica. What do we do first?"

"I am newly single, so where are the nude men?" Dydbie teased. "I hope they are all tanned and have big triceps."

"The ink is still wet on your divorce," Lyneil chastised, "and all you can think about is single men. Yes, it is all about you now, so have some fun. It is well-deserved. But be careful, girl. You seem to be the type of woman to attract a Donald Trump type who would walk up and grab you by the pu—y because he does not know how to communicate. You never want to date another man who objectifies women."

Dydbie laughed. "After a long marriage to a sadistic white-collar criminal, it may be a long time before I trust another man. I am a born-again virgin until God heals me and says otherwise."

"So, at the nude beach, are you going to close your eyes and not look at triceps?"

"We put a man who do not respect women in the white house, and we are talking about naked butts?" Sadie Mae commented. "Well, I don't want to see a gang of naked butts jumping around the beach."

"Oh, let it go, Sadie Mae," Benita said. "You might as well open both eyes because I doubt your husband will have his eyes closed while you are out of town. He will be like a bull in a china shop."

"Benita, you are so insensitive," Sadie Mae whined. "With Trump in the white house, crimes again women will increase."

"I am sorry, Sadie Mae, I fight every day for women in America. Right now, though, we are on vacation. Let's get into our rooms and change into our swimsuits and hit the pool.

Sadie Mae threw a wadded-up napkin and hit Benita. "I would get up and slap you right now, but I am too excited. Yes, we are on vacation. I can't wait to put this hot body into my blue dental floss.

"Please keep all that under wraps, big girl," Lyneil teased. "We don't want to apologize about too much booty in too little swimwear."

Sadie Mae stuck out her lower lip. "Don't hate me because I am bodacious and curvaceous, you're a skinny witch. In other words, white girl, I am beautiful."

"Yes," Dydbie said, "You are booty-full!"

"Alright, girls," Benita interceded. "Bring on your best swimsuits and your sexiest walks. The one who gets the most attention wins. The loser buys dinner tonight. I will teach you some respect."

Benita added, "Love you two," as the limo pulled up to the hotel.

They all rushed upstairs to their rooms to dress and meet in the lobby.

When the ladies approached the pool area, they put their plan into action.

"I am first," Lyneil said, wearing a white string bikini. She strutted across the pool deck and nine guys sat up and looked over their sunglasses. Their heads followed her around the pool.

By: Willi Ray

"I counted twenty people with the little boys eating ice cream," laughed Dydbie. "I think she scared the baby."

"Let me show you how it's done," Benita said. In her lemon yellow, French-cut one-piece with built-in push-up bra, she strutted the length of the pool stopped and leaned forward, the bra struggling to contain her glory. Thirty-five men stood up and moved closer to get a better view. One man introduced himself, his eyes glued to her breasts.

"I couldn't help but notice how lovely you are," he said. "Can I buy you a drink?"

Benita smiled coyly. "Yes, thank you."

Lyneil objected. "No, but thank you, sir. She is hanging with the ladies tonight."

"Lyneil!" Benita chided as Lyneil led her away. "You're mad because I got more attention than you."

"No, I am saving you from a beat down from the angry white chick we saw him talking to every since we arrived here," Lyneil laughed. "Come on, home wrecker. Yes, Queen Bea, that kind of attention is going to get you divorced."

Sadie Mae came walking past the two ladies; the smell of her perfume got their attention. When they realized it was Sadie Mae, they stood there speechless, witnessing Sadie Mae's seductive charm go to work. She looked over her shoulder, winked, and smiled. A one-piece black and white swimsuit accented her waist and breasts. She moved slowly and gracefully toward the beach.

The water was clear blue without a single cloud as if the sky and the ocean were one. Sadie Mae stopped near the lapping waves and the cool breeze made her sheer black wrap dance, hugging and caressing her body. As it blew, her silhouette seemed more defined. She looked like an angel in flight. The sun gave her face a perfect golden glow. It was a rare moment of the earth elements appreciating the essence of a woman.

Removing her sunglasses, she noticed she had everyone's attention— even the women. Her skin was flawless without a single stretch mark from the birth of her two sons. Legs were as taut and toned as Tina Turner's. Her stomach was flat and when she moved, her muscles perfectly supported her

38Ds. A 28-inch waist crowned her 40-inch apple-shaped bottom which was well-contained in her swimsuit.

The men nearby took notice and stood as if they knew Sadie Mae was performing for their attention. One man shouted, "Well done, beautiful lady." Another said, "I have to buy my wife that suit; please tell me where you bought it. You make a blind man want to sell his soul for a sight of your beautiful."

Lyneil started counting as the men approached Sadie Mae offering compliments and conversation. "I can't believe that many men find her attractive. Fifty-five! Wow!"

When Sadie Mae returned from the water's edge, Lyneil said, "What kind of mind-boggling scheme did you just pull, Sadie Mae? I don't know how you cast a spell over all those men to make them think you are hot. But at midnight the spell will be broken and you will fade back into the big-booty lady we all know and love."

"Don't make me slap you, witch," said Sadie Mae.

"Fifty-five! Wow!" Benita joined in. "Did you count those men by the pool? Dydbie cannot win this thing. Sadie Mae did one of her college numbers to us. She knows how to get attention."

"Well, in college all she had to do was walk by and guys groveled like dogs," Lyneil agreed. "She's got some kind of sex appeal."

Dydbie had to admit Sadie Mae gave them all some stiff competition, but she had not yet made her appeal. She pulled the red silk ribbon from her hair and let it flow down her back. Checked her candy-red lipstick and put her sunglasses on her head to hold her hair in place. Looking down at her brown and red four-inch Prada high-heeled sandals, she found the right angle to the light of the sun and walked in direction. She was wearing a teeny weenie red bikini with the face of an angel and the body of a Barbie doll.

With her radiant skin and captivating smile, some photographers called her the famous model a little slice of heaven; others called her the next Twiggy. She put on her best runway walk and strutted around the pool. She bent slowly to take off her shoes and walked barefoot over the white sand beach. When she dipped into the gleaming water, it beaded on her skin like crystal raindrops, her hair laid perfectly in place, adding more seduction to her persona. She walked away from the ocean, sand covering and releasing her feet with every step. Her kind of rare simplicity and girl-next-door beauty

By: Willi Ray

commanded the attention of everyone within range.

Needless to say, Dydbie won the bet. They all ran to her side and said, "We underestimated you."

"As a professional model, you have developed the skills to get those great shots," Lyneil admitted. "So much for the idea swimwear shots are all photography tricks."

"You got mad skills, girl!" Sadie Mae agreed. "You are the only one who can steal my thunder and not have a word said. You know that red bikini worked this beach today."

Lyneil added, "Yeah, we need to frame that red bikini. It's smoking hot! Si' fumare caldo, caldo!"

"Can you teach me to walk?" Benita asked.

Sadie Mae added, "I like when she came up out of the water, she threw her hair back and posed for fifteen seconds."

Lyneil caught a glint from something nearby. "The photographer snapped your picture. I hope it doesn't get into the wrong paper."

"Let me handle this," Benita said. She walked over to the photographer and asked, "Do you have a business card on you? Where can I get a copy of those pictures?"

He gave Benita his card, but said, "These pictures are not for sale to the public."

"Oh, really?" Benita touched his arm alluringly. "Okay, I will buy that camera with the negatives in it."

"No, you won't!" He pulled away from her. "Get out of here, lady. Isn't that the Senator's wife?"

Benita paused. "Let me put it another way. Here is my card. If this picture shows up anywhere I will sue you, your mother, and the company you work for. I will cancel your registration in all the hotels in Jamaica and have Big Roscoe come and take your passport and kick your skinny white butt. And it is not enough, wait until you see what I do to your criminal record."

"But I don't have a criminal record," the photographer responded.

" wait until you see what crimes you are capable of," she said calmly, "such as robbing a Federal Reserve Bank and threatening National Security."

She pulled out her cell phone and punched in the speed-dial to the hotel front desk. "Hello, my name is Attorney Benita Porter," she said. "I am investigating a homicide, and we think the fugitive is hiding in your hotel. I need to speak with the manager."

After a brief pause, she continued, "Sir, I am Attorney Benita Porter. I may need to cancel a reservation pending a criminal investigation. We are investigating a photographer, a Ralph Bluebush. Until further notice, he is under observation."

The Photographer, realizing he was dealing with a powerful woman who meant business, gave her the camera, stalked away, and shouted over his shoulder, "You will hear from my lawyer."

"Be careful, picture man," Benita called after him, "you are outmatched. Watch yourself."

With a chuckle, Benita called the hotel manager again. "About the murder, we need to do more investigation on this matter. Mr. Bluebush is not our suspect after all. Thank you."

Benita called to the photographer, "Hey, you forgot something." She pulled several bills from her bag. "Here is $500 and a tip: Take a good look at my friends. Never take pictures of me and my friends again or there will be hell to pay. When will you crumb snatchers learn you can destroy someone's life for a buck?"

She shook his hand and walked away.

When Benita returned to her friends, Sadie Mae, eyes big with amazement, asked, "What did you say to him to make him give up that camera?"

"I offered him $500. He took it and thanked me."

"So, he recognized Dydbie," Lyneil said. "You are so good with people."

"Thanks, Bea," Dydbie added. "I will give you the money. You are such a good friend."

"What are friends for, if not to protect each other?"

Chapter 8

"So, losers," Dydbie chided, "where are we going for dinner?"

"You and Sadie Mae are stiff competition for each other," Benita said.

Lyneil said, "Well, since I am buying dinner, my dinner guests must be dressed a certain way."

Sadie Mae rolled her eyes. "We should all know Lyneil is going to punish us because she lost, just so you know."

"Yes, Lyneil," Dydbie added, "we are not falling for any of your shenanigans. You have never been a graceful loser."

Benita asked calmly, "Okay, what are we wearing? Lyn, be nice."

Looking out of the corner of her eye and stifling a grin, Lyneil said, "You all are being babies. I am your girl and I've got your best interests at heart. Trust me, I will send your dresses to your rooms. I have matured since college and I am not going to seek revenge. I am good; trust me. See you all later. But first, I have to take care of something."

She walked away, dialing her phone. "Information? Can I get the number to a costume store? You have dresses that glow in the dark? What time do you close? Five p.m.? Great! I am on my way now."

Lyneil found the dresses she was looking for and took them to the front desk along with detailed instructions. "Please deliver these dresses to these rooms," she told the clerk. "ASAP."

Lyneil called Benita. "Where are you all now?"

"SAX Fifth Avenue at the mall."

"I am going for a swim. I made reservations at this wonderful Jamaican restaurant. When are we going to work on Sadie Mae's problem?"

"We will talk with her tomorrow. That is, if we survive the night with you."

"You all are in loving hands with me."

Benita wondered. "See you in an hour."

By 6:00pm all the ladies were in their rooms, getting ready for dinner. As each opened their wardrobe bag, the dress they found there looked pretty and stylish. They showered, fixed their hair, and put on makeup. They slipped into their gowns. Benita's dress was sky blue. Dydbie's was mint green, and Sadie Mae's was light pink. Each included shoes to match. They all walked into a well-lit restaurant, each in a dress of their favorite color.

"These dresses are beautiful," Sadie Mae glowed happily. "Thank you, Lyn. If you kill us, we will be well-dressed corpses." Everyone laughed.

"Benita, you owe Lyneil an apology," Dydbie added. "You said to watch her tonight because she is a sore loser. Just because she was a witch in college doesn't mean she has not changed."

"Maybe I was wrong," Benita admitted, "but my gut still tells me Lyn is a sore loser, and we will pay for it tonight."

"Ladies," Lyneil said, "let's have dinner and after that we can dance and talk. The night is young. Don't let Benita's paranoia spoil the evening."

Dydbie nodded in the direction of a gentleman across the room. "Hey, isn't that Paul, Sadie Mae's prom date?" she asked.

"Please, don't repeat that," Sadie Mae hissed through her teeth. "My husband may get wind of it and there would be hell to pay."

Indeed, Paul was winding his way across to their table. He said to Sadie, "I wondered if I would ever see you again. I love your persona. I thought about you all day, and kept telling myself you are a happily married woman, right?"

Sadie Mae smiled tensely. "Yes, I am. Did Benita invite you here?"

Benita nudged Sadie Mae with her elbow.

"Paul, are you here on pleasure or business?" Benita asked.

By: Willi Ray

Behind Paul, Lyneil looked at Sadie Mae, making kissing gestures. Paul turned to see what Sadie Mae was looking at.

Lyneil quickly straightened her face. "Hi, Paul. Good to see you again. You here alone?"

Paul replied, "No, my lady friend and I needed to get away, so we thought about Jamaica."

Sadie Mae's face dropped a little. Being reminded of how handsome he was, she had drifted away to fantasy land for a second. What a beautiful hunk of male specimen he was.

"I see my friend coming," Paul said, pulling Sadie Mae out of her daydream. "I will talk to you all later. Tell your husband how lucky he is to have found you before I did."

"Paul, thank you for noticing," Sadie Mae said. "I am a woman and I need to be told I am still attractive. Please do me a favor; never stop loving that special person in your life like you did when you loved her for the first time. It is a motivator. True love is one of the most important things in life, yet we use it as a sports game. I believe after and only after we as human beings have exhausted every possibility to save our love, we should give up the fight. I would walk away before giving in to cheating and mind games. That's me, Paul."

"Sadie Mae, I am here if you need to talk. I am good at listening, and I have a broad shoulder and a handkerchief if you need one. I would never make a play for you unless you were ready." Paul turned to go. "See you ladies later. As always, I am amazed to see so much beauty in one place, you all complement each other." He kissed Sadie Mae on the cheek and walked away with a wave to the others.

During Sadie Mae and Paul's conversation, Lyneil teased Benita, "'Lucy, you have some 'splaining to do.' Why do these men keep popping up in the strangest places? Did you see the attraction between him and Sadie Mae?"

Dydbie whispered, "Yes, but a threesome is an inconvenient complication in a marriage." Laughing, she added, "She must repent for the lust in her heart."

"Lord knows we do not need any more stumbling blocks in these rocky-road marriages," Lyneil moaned. "Sadie Mae is committed to her marriage until all hope is gone."

"Yeah, I hate to see her hurting so bad," Benita said quietly. "She has been kind of distant lately. But she is the type of wife who will ride the wagon until the wheels fall off."

Dydbie whispered, "Yesterday in the bathroom stall I heard a heated argument between her and her husband. It was not over the boys. I think maybe it was about how he treats her. I did hear her say, 'I am not overweight or fat,' she sighed and hung up the phone."

"Girl, she has gained forty pounds during the marriage," Lyneil commented. "At least she gained the weight after giving birth to two babies."

"Let's cheer her up," Benita said. "When we go to the club later, how about asking the owner if she can sit in on one of his jazz sets?"

Dydbie agreed that was a great idea. "She loves to sing. What song should we request for her to do? I love it when Sadie Mae closes her eyes and sings. She elevates everyone's souls in the room. Yes, her voice can make angels in flight stop to listen."

The Jazz club was packed with excitement, the ladies found their seat and the waiter brought a bottle of Araujo Eisele Red Wine.

Lyneil lifted her glass. "Ladies, let's drink to solving marital problems and the forgiveness of good friends."

The lights went down; enhancing the romantic setting and the band played sexy, flirty music. After a few pieces, the band leader called Sadie Mae to come sit in with the band.

Sadie Mae stood up, surprised and excited. "Oh, my goodness, did they call my name? I don't know anything to sing. I am enjoying the music." To the band, she called, "Play on, please. Band, play on."

Benita patted her arm. "Sadie Mae, you know how much you love to sing. Go on up there."

"Oh, okay," Sadie Mae said breathlessly. "If I embarrass myself only Jamaica will see it." She walked up to the bandstand, and they played Anita Baker's, "What's wrong."

Sadie Mae turned her head to the left, cleared her throat, took a

By: Willi Ray

deep breath, and stepped to the mic. Her mood and body changed. As her contralto voice flowed through the mic, it seemed to captivate the room. A hush fell on the audience. Everyone stopped their conversations and gave their full attention to the singer at the mic.

Sadie Mae was into her second song. Her body swayed to Anita Baker's "Sweet Love." Mentally, she had crossed over into her sexy, seductive, comfort zone. The heat elevation from the hot sweaty, sultry voice vibrations caused her dress to change forms. It glowed in the dark, and shrink! Sadie Mae did not know what was going on because her eyes were closed. When she hit the high notes, the room burst into applause as if the glowing of the shrinking dress were part of the act.

Lyneil screamed with laughter. She got up and moved away from the other ladies.

The crowd went crazy as the long, formal gown climbed up Sadie Mae's thighs.

"Ladies, look at Sadie Mae's dress," Benita said. "It is so—bright."

"And so short!" added Dydbie. "Where is Lyneil? There she is over there by the stage, pointing and laughing. I told you not to trust her."

Benita was angry. "We are going to kill her later. But if we do not get Sadie Mae off stage she will be wearing nothing in a few minutes."

When the girls stood to go get Sadie Mae, Lyneil snapped pictures of Benita's and Dydbie's shrinking dresses.

Paul appeared beside Benita. "Is there a wardrobe problem?" he asked with some alarm. "Is this part of her act? I can almost see—"

Benita stopped him. "Come on. We have got to get her off stage. I will explain later."

"Afterwards," Dydbie added, "we are going to kill Lyneil."

"Lyn!" Benita grabbed her. "Look what you've done."

"You guys are sore losers," laughed Lyneil. "Can't you all take a joke?"

Red in the face, Benita looked at Dydbie and yelled, "We are all glowing in the dark!"

"Yes, my dress is moving up my ankles," Dydbie screamed. "Woo! You are going to get it, Lyn!"

"What the hell is going on?" Paul interjected. "Is my suit glowing in the dark?" He walked over to the mirror to check himself.

"Oopa!" howled Lyneil. "Keep it coming, ladies. The more heat your bodies create the shorter your dresses will get!"

Benita and Dydbie both rushed onto the stage. "Sadie Mae, open your eyes," Benita whispered. "Don't panic, but you are almost naked."

" slowly fade into the background," Dydbie added, "and we will take the stage."

Sadie Mae stopped singing and quickly stepped back with the band members' eyes following her off the stage. They were confused. They looked at Benita and Dydbie, whose dresses were halfway up their thighs.

Paul took the mic to sing the last verse of "Sweet Love."

"Who knew he could sing?" whispered Dydbie to Benita.

When he finished singing, Paul whispered, "Lyneil is backstage with three robes."

Everyone in the room stood, clapping and screaming, "More, More, More!" The band singer stepped to the mic and started a dance tune. Soon everyone in the club filled the dance floor.

Backstage, tempers were flaring. Paul quickly stepped between Lyneil and the others.

"Lower your voices, ladies," Paul whispered loudly while refereeing. He feared if they got their hands on Lyneil, they would hurt her. "I am sure Lyneil can explain if you give her a chance."

"After she gets my foot out her butt," Sadie Mae hissed. "To be clear, I am going to kill her."

Dydbie pulled her hair back into a ponytail and removed her earrings

By: Willi Ray

and her shoes. "Get in line behind me, Sadie Mae."

Benita chimed in. "There will be nothing left to kill when I am done. I am going to murder her!" She lunged toward Lyneil, but Paul blocked her.

Lyneil pleaded, "I am sorry things got out of control. I had you all's backs. I said I was sorry, please don't hurt me. I am sorry. Sono spiacente non mi duole. Per favore sono spiacente."

"I am going to whip your skinny narrow butt!" Sadie Mae said, pawing to get past Paul.

Lyneil started to cry. "I said I am sorry. I will never do anything like this again. Can't we all get along?"

"Yes," Dydbie said, "right after this beat down."

Benita broke into loud laughter. "Lyneil, I don't know if those tears are real or not, but you better be glad Paul was here because we were going to murder you."

It caused them all to relax and laugh. All except Sadie Mae.

Sadie Mae was somewhere between embarrassment and tears. She was so angry she could barely get words out of her mouth. "I cannot tell you how surprised I was when I opened my eyes and my dress was way up my thighs. I am so glad no one in the States will ever see this. You went too far this time, Lyneil. I have to admit this was the joke of the century, but to be clear, I will hurt you terribly bad next time. You got it?"

Finally, she couldn't help smiling. That was Lyneil's best prank yet.

Early Sunday morning, Benita called the front desk. "I need a private room for brunch for four ladies. How soon can you set this up?" The hotel staff assured her it would be ready in an hour.

Next Benita called the courthouse in Hawaii to check on the court date for Lyneil's divorce and the date for her suit against her husband's girlfriend. She was told both had been served and the court date was September 15.

Benita called the ladies and told them they were to meet for brunch in the private room, so they could discuss Sadie Mae's problem. They were all there eating and laughing when Lyneil's phone rang.

It was her husband. He was upset and calling her all kinds of names. He yelled, "I dare you sue me for something you have no proof of. Leave Cindy out of this. This is between me and you. Did you have her car repossessed? You listen to me, Lyn—" was the last thing Lyneil heard before she laughed and hung up.

"I take it he has been served," Benita said.

"Yes. What a wonderful day it is. I did not know the woman's name was Cindy. It sounded like she is having some car trouble. I am glad I live in Hawaii," she paused, thinking. "Benita, he said I can't do anything without proof. What am I going to do? I am suing this man for cheating without proof. I am going to look like a fool in court. You are my lawyer. Do something."

"Lyn, enjoy your lunch," Benita laughed. "We will plan our strategy. Trust your lawyer and friend. I've got things under control."

Sadie Mae commented, "He is one mad black man. I could hear him yelling through the phone. What's done in the dark will come to light. Most men never think they will get caught. Cheating is a woman's game. We can bring home the bacon—stop by and see Tom, Dick or Harry—fry it up in a pan, and never, ever let him forget he's a man. Oh, yeah, cheating is a woman's game. I don't cheat because it's beneath me. I am smart enough not to call my husband and yell at him about my other man."

"You reap what you sow," Dydbie concluded. "I hope she was worth it because it is going to cost him big money. He should win the TSTC award."

Lyneil asked, "What's TSTC?"

"Too Stupid to Cheat Award."

"It is not true women can cheat better than men. The fact is, a woman cheating is more serious than a man cheating. You see, women are emotional creatures. When a woman cheats, she gives parts of herself to that man. She gives her body, her mind, her feelings, and she is emotionally attached, whereas men can walk away with no emotional attachment."

Lyneil's phone rang again, and again, it was her husband. "What are you crying about now, man?"

By: Willi Ray

"I know you had something to do with the police arresting Cindy for prostitution," he yelled. "If you did, you better hope I never find out."

Lyneil's laughter was filled with gratification. At least this one time, justice had been served. She chuckled one last time, and she said, "Do not call me again. It's not my fault the hooker you are sleeping with got arrested for doing her job. Maybe you should ask for your money back and get an HIV test, fool. Did you think because she is white you didn't need to protect yourself? I cannot believe you exposed me to what she might be carrying around in her line of work. Do not let those AIDS statistics fool you. HIV and AIDS are not selective. It is a whosoever game out there." She hung up.

They all laughed.

"What's wrong with him?" Sadie Mae asked. "Now it's your fault he is sleeping with a prostitute with a warrant on her head? Girl, he is stupid, and he shows you total disrespect. You need to handle your business."

Sadie Mae opened her mouth to continue, and all the ladies shouted in unison, "To be clear—" and they laughed together.

"Oh, you all got jokes," Sadie Mae said. "But this man has a real problem with simplicity and stupidity."

Dydbie looked at Lyneil. "How many men calls their wives up and yell at her because the girlfriend went to jail for prostitution? What's going on?" She laughed. "Men playing the games."

"Well, this time I recorded the phone call since he said I have no proof. This white girl chased down a black man who gave her a bad case of the blues. I bet she wants to run for cover, let's see if she runs for cover now. Maybe women who date married men should find out what the wife is like before they enter into the deep."

Lyneil's phone rang again. Sadie Mae took the phone from her.

"Lyn, you did have her car repossessed," Mr. Gazella ranted into the phone. "I got a call from the finance company about it. Cindy took her mother to the store and when she came out, her car was going down the street on a truck. Lyn, I did not finance that car for her. My company bought the car and raffled it off. She won it. Why are you terrorizing her? She is a friend. Leave her the hell alone. Lyn, give the woman back her car. Where are you, Lyn? You haven't been home in months. Let's talk about this, Lyn. Why do you want a divorce? We can work this out. We are still married."

Sadie Mae lit into him. "Wow, they say men don't get emotional. Slow down, liar. Listen, Bro-man, I am trying to respect you but, LOL, man, I hope you have a good lawyer. Most intelligent men do not bring the problems they are having with their whores to their wives' doors. Isn't there supposed to be some deniability in the busy intersection of marriage? I know you failed Basic Cheater 101. Honey, you need to go get your money back." She laughed and hung up the phone.

In a few seconds, Mr. Gazella called back. "Who is this? Put Lyn on the phone."

Sadie Mae laughed into the phone and hung up again.

Lyneil's stomach was trembling from the tension. She stood and paced. "He is giving me credit for things I haven't done yet. So, let me wrap my mind around this thing. He financed a car for this woman, and he thinks we can work out our marital problems? He has lost his mind." She started spouting fast Italian. "Stupid male whore. Puttana stupida maschia. Who does he think he is? I am nobody's fool. This is ignorant, stupid, underdeveloped male ego. Fool, foolish crazy man. Chi pensa che e'? Non sono l'alcun sciocco. Questo e' Ignorante, Stupido sotto il develope l'ego maschino. Ingannare l'uomo Stupido matto!"

"Hush, Lyn," Benita said. "Let him sweat for a while. And get rid of that phone. You don't need this kind of stress." She took Lyn's phone and put it in her own purse. "Your court date is September 15th. Save the talking for the judge."

Clapping her hands together to get the ladies' attention, Benita concluded, "Okay, ladies, we need to help Sadie Mae. So, Sadie Mae, how can we help? We can listen and loan you a shoulder to cry on IF this is what you need."

"Well," Sadie Mae said cautiously, "my husband Michael has been riding me about losing weight. He calls me 'fat girl' and tells his friends I don't care about myself anymore. He said the reason we do not go out anymore is because he is ashamed of being seen with a fat woman. Saying all his friends have hot wives, and he is stuck with Old Mother Hubbard. Ladies, he is brutal.

By: Willi Ray

It would not hurt so badly if I did not love him so much."

"Sadie Mae, how do you feel about your weight?" Lyneil asked. "Do you want to lose weight? I tease you a lot, but girlfriend, I wish I had some curves like you have. Tell us how you are taking the verbal abuse. When did it start?"

" Just to be clear," Sadie Mae began, "I am mad as hell, because I gave this man two sons and now he disrespects me like this. He thinks he can talk to me any kind of way, as if being fat means I have no feelings."

She paused to get her thoughts together. "Yes, when we got married and decided to have children we both knew there was a great possibility I would not lose all the weight. My second child put more weight on me than the first one. I sacrificed my body for nine months giving him each of those boys. I was on bed rest for the last two months of the second pregnancy."

"Girl—" Dydbie interrupted.

"No, no, now I know what you are going to say. It's true; I have not lost all the weight. But after all, he doesn't love me anymore? Am I not worthy of love because I am fat? What the hell. And he thinks I am to blame for our marriage being so bad. I am five-feet-eight and I weigh 160 pounds. I do not feel I am too fat to be loved. He promised to love me for better or for worse. But weight gained during childbirth is a deal breaker?"

"How old is your youngest son?" Benita asked.

"My baby Keith is three years old."

"Let's get real," said Dydbie. "Will losing the weight save the marriage or is this the tip of the iceberg for bigger problems hidden behind your weight gain? Men are never straightforward about their feelings."

"I don't know. But I am so angry he feels he can't love me unless I am a size four or six. I thought love hides a multitude of faults."

"If you want to lose weight, stop whining and lose the weight," Benita interjected. "But do you want to lose it for him or for you? Sadie Mae, there are some people who believe weight gain is a ticket to cheat in a relationship. It is important to understand his mindset."

Sadie Mae looked at Benita. "This is not about the weight. It is more about control. I was going to lose the weight months ago but I did not want to have him think I lost it for him. I will lose it when I get ready, and not to gain a superficial love from a man who has lost sight of me as a person. He said he cannot love me because fat people are not worthy of love. I refuse to play his game. Besides, he has gained 40 pounds since we got married. I love him enough to look beyond his weight and see the man I love.

"In his eyes, being a thick girl—chucky, overweight, heavy, fat, plus-sized, obese, whatever the term is—means no respect. We are still human and deserve to be treated with courtesy. Respect me! Don't respect me because I am hot. No, respect me because I gave you two sons. Respect me because I am your wife. Respect me because I am a woman and a mother."

"Respect!" all the ladies shouted in unison. Sadie Mae looked at them, smiled, and continued preaching.

"I did not stop being me nor did I become the butt of America's jokes because I am considered fat. No, I am a beautiful woman with feelings and real emotions. I can't believe the man I love can look me in my face and tell me he cannot make love to a fat woman because the extra weight is a turn off. Who does he think he is? Suppose I told him not to worry because there is little to miss. If he wants me to lose the weight, he needs to treat me better. He should ask me to lose the weight and be supportive. Don't bully and threaten me. I don't respond well to threats. I am from the South Side of Chicago and I will break him off a piece of whip ---."

"Okay, Sadie Mae, we get you," Benita said. "I can tell this hurts you deeply. I personally think you look great. But I have an idea. Men are visual creatures and we will deal with it. How do you feel about wearing a fat suit? It will make you look like you have gained an additional fifteen pounds. So, if he thinks you are disgusting now, wait until he sees you on Monday."

"If I come home fatter than when I left he will have a stroke."

"This is going to be fun," Dydbie laughed. "Bea, you mean to tell me we are going to make her fatter and send her home to a man who want to be like the Jones? If Sadie Mae comes up missing, we will know who did it. I would love to be a fly on the wall when Sadie Mae walks in looking fatter than she was before she came on this trip."

"Give him a big eye-opener. If he doesn't like you now, you can always get fatter. You don't have to wear the fat suit to work, just at home, but in the meantime, you will lose twenty pounds."

"Well," Benita concluded, changing the mood, "We will finish this conversation later. I chartered us a yacht for a party tonight."

"Will those fine guys we met in Atlanta be there tonight?" Lyneil asked.

Benita smiled. "Yes, Paul with be there. His sister flew home today."

"Inquiring minds," Sadie Mae teased. "So, you knew the lady was his sister?"

Dydbie laughed and sat forward in her black leather chair. "Down, girl. We are working to fix the mess you are in now. So, let Paul rest for a while. I saw the way he looks at you. He is off limits. Sadie Mae, when was the last time you made love to your husband?"

"Dydbie, don't try to be funny said Sadie Mae. Yes, I am in bad shape right now. I can't pray away this feeling of needing the comfort of my man. I can't wish away this need to be loved. I wake up at night missing his touch and I cry myself to sleep. I cannot remember the last time he made love to me. When morning comes, he rolls over, I say good morning, as he walks into the shower, and that starts another day of empty painful marriage. Love hurts when it is filled with confusion. Marriage is hard when he is pulling one way, and she is struggling to hold it together. When he ignores me and when he is not calling me fat, those are the moments I have hope that God will help us. I say, God sees this, and he will guide us through the darkness. And other days I am so distrustful that our good life has turned into a place of hell."

"Paul is a gentleman," Benita concluded. "He will not take advantage of Sadie Mae. We don't know about Sadie Mae's desire for love. We will protect you from you, Sadie Mae."

"Paul is hot," Sadie Mae replied.

"Oh, my goodness!" Dydbie laughed.

"Okay, ladies, we are our sister's keeper, so be on guard tonight." Benita turned to Sadie Mae. "We are all having a spa treatment in an hour. Hopefully that will help you relax. Dydbie, picked out our outfits for the party."

Sadie Mae snickered. "I am stilling having nightmares about the dresses Lyneil picked out. The world was about to see my glory. It is funny now, but it wasn't funny in the moment."

"Tell me, Sadie Mae, you did have on underwear?" Dydbie asked.

"I didn't," Benita interjected. "That's why I was going to murder Lyn."

Lyneil laughed. "I said I was sorry. But you guys have to admit, it was a perfectly good joke, carried out to perfection. The problem was, you guys did not respect my skill set. All you did was cry."

They all stared at Lyneil. "Okay, it is time to kill her," Benita charged.

"Get her!" Sadie Mae screamed. Lyneil ran and they all followed her. She got to her room and inside before they caught her.

Sadie Mae called through the door, "You have to come out sometime tonight!"

Benita added, "We are going to let this go for now. It was funny as hell. See you later on the big boat."

They all took a cab to the boat. The party was already going when they boarded. Benita had invited several large law firms in Jamaica. Dydbie had invited people and organizations located in Jamaica in her modeling circle. Lyneil had invited top business executives. Sadie Mae had invited publishers and authors associated with her publisher. The yacht sailed the crystal-clear water under the blue sky, gentle breezes seemingly from the four directions, north, south, east, and west. The boat floated across the sea with ease. The music was jumping and the people were enjoying themselves, the dance floor was full of excitement. Sadie Mae spotted Paul, and she made a bee line in his direction.

"Follow her," Lyneil prompted the others. She caught Sadie Mae's elbow. "Hey, aren't you hanging with the girls tonight?"

"I need male company tonight," Sadie Mae answered. "I am so tired of being ignored by my husband. He is supposed to meet my needs, but he punishes me for being overweight. I am only human, Lyn. Can I get some space to breathe? I will not do anything more than what my husband is doing wherever he is tonight."

By: Willi Ray

Lyneil squeezed her arm. "Sadie Mae, I will give you some space but don't do anything you cannot take back. Life is full of uncontrollable things, but we as women have to stay above the expectation of justification."

"Lyn, I love you but go away now. I promise I will not leave this room."

"How about a cold glass of wine? It will help you feel better. Paul is coming your way."

Paul joined them and asked if he could get them a drink. "Sadie Mae, you prefer red wine, right?"

"Yes, Paul. Thanks."

Lyneil kissed Paul on the cheek and walked away.

After a few sips of wine, Paul asked, "Do you want to dance, pretty lady?"

"Paul, you are a welcome sight. Yes, I want to dance. Where is your sister?"

"She is socializing. She will be fine in a room full of men, which is why I found you so fast. I want all your attention tonight."

Before Paul had completed his sentence, another man walked up and asked Sadie Mae for her autograph. "Are you singing tonight?" he asked.

Sadie Mae blushed a little. "No, and I am not a famous singer."

"I know," the man responded. "I bought your last book of love poems. I enjoy reading it. I would like to talk to you about it sometime tonight."

Paul interrupted. "She owes me the first dance and if she wants she can talk to you."

He turned his back toward the other man. "Sadie Mae, it is nice to see your eyes lit up as big and wide as the sky. This black dress you are wearing is so beautiful. I hope Lyneil did not pick it out. I would like to have a nice evening filled with dancing and romancing and no disappearing evening dress laugh Sadie Mae"

The other man persisted. "Sorry to interrupt," he said to Paul. "I wanted to meet Ms. Crenshaw. I am a big fan of her work."

Paul took Sadie Mae by the hand and led her to the dance floor. "After I met you three months ago, I went out and bought every book you have written. I enjoyed *Stop the World I Want to Get Off* most, I think. That book is so profound. Where did you get your research? Whoa, you blew me away with your righteous thought process. I also loved *If You Ask Me* and *Color Me Happy*. *Color Me Happy II* made me take inventory of my life and my dreams. Sadie Mae, I love your mind."

"Paul, you make me feel so good. Now move those feet."

Paul laughed. "My feet are lethal. I love to dance. You try to keep up."

They danced and walked out onto the deck of the boat. The sun was going down and the moon had claimed her place in the sky. The stars sparkled like a cluster of the expensive diamonds worn by most of the women at the party.

It was like a grand ball on the yacht. Dydbie had dressed the ladies in the most expensive gowns, designed by Carolina Herrera. She had borrowed diamonds from her favorite jewelers and flown in her favorite hairdresser to do everyone's hair and makeup. Yes, tonight the ladies looked filthy rich. They had everything but escorts. So, Benita had invited the guys again—Luke, Allen, and Kendal.

Allen had it bad for Benita but did not want to show it out of mutual respect for their friendship. He had been waiting and hoping whenever her dying marriage fell apart he could be her knight in shining armor. He checked in by email from time to time, to say "how are you," hoping one day he would be first on the scene to pick up the pieces.

Luke was in love with the persona Dydbie presented, a beautiful, hardworking woman who was married but never had a husband. He wanted to show her what a real man looked and felt like.

Kendal was the only one there with no personal motive. He was there because Benita invited him. He knew Lyneil was married, so he safely guarded his heart.

Benita did not know her husband Raheem was also making a surprise appearance.

When Lyneil saw Kendal, she forgot about keeping an eye on Sadie Mae. She hoped to get his attention and waited to see if he would notice her.

By: Willi Ray

Kendal caught her eye and approached the group. "Hello, lovely ladies. It's so nice to see you all again." To Lyneil, "How is the hubby?"

"Well, that is a good question. You see, I live in Hawaii now. But I am not here to talk about my husband."

Kendal nodded his head. "I get a sense of the danger before I decide if I can stand my ground and fight."

"Come on in and enjoy the party," Lyneil said. "There is no danger. There is only me."

"I am careful because when a man has a beautiful wife, he will fight to protect his domain."

"Relax, solider. Put your guns away. No one thinks I am worth fighting for."

Kendal disagreed. "Beautiful, intelligent, professional, and sexy? That's a winning hand to any self-respecting man. Most men look for eye candy but professional men look for the total package woman. A man wants the type of woman that will fit into his world with the greatest of ease. Secretly, he wants his friends to envy him and desire her even though they will never be able to have her."

"Kendal, what is the total package in your professional opinion? You see, I thought most of you hardworking men wanted a submissive, simpleminded step-and-fetch-it type of woman, a woman who is dependent upon her man for everything because she makes less money. You all also want the big round butted, balloon chested, empty-headed Barbie with the IQ of a gnat; white or black, it does not matter as long as she is stupid."

"Do I detect a sense of hostility in your tone? I see you are a ball-kicker," Kendal laughed. "You are hard on the male gender. Yes, we are visual creatures of habit, but I am so glad I don't fit in any of those brackets you mentioned. It sounds like some man in your life did not handle his business well. Lovely lady, shall we dance? You need to relax."

"I am not hostile," Lyneil protested. "I am unsympathetic to the black male ego, thank you."

"Have you talked to your husband about the way you feel? Black men are not the only ones who treat women similarly. Maybe you should get some counseling."

"I've got the answer to my situation. It's called divorce. We are beyond counseling. He is sleeping with a white woman."

Kendal smiled. "Correction—he is sleeping with another woman. Her color is not the issue; his infidelity is your problem. Come on. Let me get you into the party mood. Smile. You are still the most amazing and prettiest woman in this room. Cinderella, may I have this dance? Promise me you will not let this stuff make you bitter against all men."

"Sure, Prince Charming. Now move those feet."

As Kendal and Lyneil moved onto the dance floor, Luke arrived. "Hello, Dydbie. I was hoping to see you again. I rescheduled all my patients for the next three days when I got the call from Bea."

Dydbie laughed. "How is that right hook doing? I never got a chance to thank you. You have no idea how happy I was to see you that day. You're not all work and no play, is you, Mister Be-the-Man?" She kissed him on the cheek.

"For you, I will."

Dydbie asked, "That is an incomplete statement or a new hang phrase?"

"It is an answer to anything you want and everything I desire. I am waiting on you to complete it."

"Yes, I will dance with you."

"Be careful," Luke warned. "It can imply a lifetime of romance or a brief joyful movement of time on the dance floor."

"Well, Dr. Philosopher, let's take it to the dance floor. Can you dance the Mambo?

"I'll let my feet answer that question. I am not good with flirting. Please let me know when I get it right."

"You had me at, 'For you, I will.'"

"So, did I get some cool points?"

The Mambo came easy to both of them. They looked like they were

By: Willi Ray

professional dance partners.

Benita looked around for her friends. She was happy to see they were all on the dance floor. Allen joined her. "Hello, Bea. This is a great party. You are looking exquisite, the most beautiful woman here. May I have this dance?"

"Yes," Benita smiled warmly.

When the dance was over, Benita and Allen walked out on the deck to get some air. Allen gave her a glass of wine as she breathed in deeply to catch her breath. She gazed at the golden sunset on the beautiful blue waters and at Allen. There was something about the way he looked at her every time they met. It was as if she was the only woman in the room. This always reassured Benita she was still beautiful.

As he spoke, Benita saw his lips moving, but her thoughts were not on his words. She was wondering if he would always think she was beautiful or, like her husband Raheem, would her beauty become invisible to him? She smiled and thought to herself, tonight, in his eyes I am beautiful. Nothing else matters tonight.

"Benita," Allen said, looking at the beauty and mystery filled the sky, "Where does beauty hide her secrets?"

"Why does beauty have so many secrets to hide?" she asked. "She could want to be appreciated and noticed."

Allen smiled, slipping his hands into his pants pockets. "Benita, I notice all the special beautiful things God put in this world to give our hearts joy. I will never forget the first time I saw you walk into the law firm with a cup of Dunkin Donuts coffee in your hand. Your hair was pulled back into a beautiful up-do. Your lips were a soft pink and you wore a pink dress and off-white stiletto heels, pearl earring, and necklace. I could tell by your strong sense of self you were somebody. I have always wondered the name of the perfume you were wearing. Now three years have gone by, and I am still in awe at the sweet smell of beauty and confidence of you."

Looking at Allen out of the corner of her eye, she now realized he was making a pass for her affections. "Allen, you have a good memory." She chose her words carefully. "I depend on you as a dear friend and I can't have you falling in love with me. Pull up, man. You are flying too low. You will crash and burn. I am a married woman."

Allen smiled. "I think it saddens God when a beautiful woman walks into the room and no one notices her. God went through a lot of trouble to create beauty and it should not go unnoticed. Bea, you are too late. I have loved you since the first time I saw you. It is not your fault I feel this way. I know you are married and I respect it."

"Allen." Benita called his name to get his full attention before making her statement again. "I know you have deep feelings for me, but I am still a married woman. The truth is, I help my girls with their problems, but I have problems of my own. My friends think I am happily married, but I am dealing with a husband who doesn't know I exist. Why do men marry for the love and beauty that they can't live without and get used to seeing it and ignore it? I call it the pretty-girl-syndrome: Buy her, take her home, and put her on the shelf with the other trophies there."

Allen chuckled. "Yes, most men have the pretty-girl-syndrome. We want and admire the best and the most beautiful woman we can find. But there are some men who still protect and care for their beautiful trophy, as you so well stated. So, do not put all men in the same category. I look deeper than the outer appearance. I want to see what the heart and soul of woman is like. I am a man, and I love pretty women. God made me with a desire for women. But I only take them one at a time. If you told me you were free today, I would drop everything in my life and pursue you with everything inside me. You are the kind of woman who makes a man feel proud and blessed to have found you. You are a rare treasure, Bea."

Benita had her back to the door of the opening to the deck of the boat, but Allen saw the tall well-dressed man approaching in their direction. At the moment, Benita's mind was on how to explain to her husband why she would not be home for their anniversary. She did not feel Raheem would remember it or even notice she was not there. She wondered if his love for her could make the adjustments as she aged, and one day became her mother. Hurting inside from the self-inflicted wounds of aging. In her mind, she wondered if she should get out of the marriage before she started to show her age. She was afraid to trust that her husband was not the red-sports-car, trophy-wife type of man, and he would love her beyond time and whatever life threw at them. So, she cut her husband off at every turn.

Raheem made eye contact with Benita. "I flew to Jamaica to celebrate our anniversary with you," he said. "Excuse me, Allen, but my wife and I need to talk. Benita, I do not know what is going on here, but I am still your husband, for better or for worse."

By: Willi Ray

Benita was surprised to see her husband. "How did you get here?"

Allen kissed Benita's hand and looked at Raheem. "See you later," he said, and shook Raheem's hand walked away.

Benita said in a low voice, "Our anniversary isn't until next week. So why are you here? You've been ignoring me for the last two years, so why is our coming anniversary so important, Raheem?"

Raheem reached for her hand. "Honey, the last time you were home you had a nightmare and I have not been able to get it out of my head. Bea, you called out in your sleep for me to help you. I had to wonder why you were lying next to me and still you did not feel safe. At first, I wondered if there was another man, but I realized, if it was the case, you wouldn't be calling for me. I asked you the next day if you needed me to help you with something and you said no. I asked about your dream, and you said you don't dream anymore."

He stroked the back of her hand with his thumb. "It bothered me you were in so much distress you let out a piercing scream in your sleep. It makes a man feel helpless if he cannot protect the ones he loves the most. Benita, I am your husband and I cannot help you if you keep shutting me out. I need to understand why you call for me at night but never ask for help during the day. I took for granted you knew how much I loved you and yes, I forget to put it into words some days, but I am here. I felt us drifting apart and I ignored it because I did not know what else to do. Bea, what's wrong with us?"

Benita looked over his shoulder, unable to process his sudden interest in her well-being. "Now you want to talk, Raheem?"

"Benita, are you having an emotional affair with Allen?"

"We are friends," she said. "We are not sexually involved."

"The initial attraction is not sexual," he said. "It's the feeling that this is someone I can talk to, or this person gets me. Benita the time you steal from us and give to him weakens us and strengthens him."

"Raheem, I am not having an emotional affair," she said. "How dare you accuse me? We are two good friends supporting each other."

"Whatever," Raheem responded. "Conversations eventually become personal and the talk turns toward relationships that both partners are currently in. Suddenly you find yourself sharing aspects of our marriage you have never talked about with me. At first it may seem a bit strange, but you tell yourself you're just talking to a friend so it is okay."

He continued, "Gradually the intensity of those conversations grows, whether in person, on the phone, texting or online, and so does the anticipation of these conversations. They become something you look forward to more than anything else during the day, more than even seeing me. And by the way, you are not sharing much about this relationship with me, not the intimate things you talk about with him. But you do find yourself less and less into our relationship. Bea, think before you answer, I have noticed you need time to talk to Allen or check your email or text messages from him and smiling while you compose your responses. No, I haven't seen you sneak out of bed to check email or text messages, but I have noticed some nights when you can't sleep you are on your phone. You say you are reading material for a case, but when I ask what's wrong with us, you tell me about this friendship with Allen and you brush off my concerns or get defensive. The distance between us has grown in the past six months, but I will not let Allen take my place in your heart of emotions. Honey, I need you and I will drop everything in this world if it means securing our foundation again."

"Raheem, men are as emotional as women are. Why do you think I am emotionally attached to Allen? He is a friend," said Benita.

"Then walk away from him, Bea."

She dropped her head. "Why am I the only one giving up my friends? What about the women you talk to?"

"If he is a friend, answer a few questions, honey. I don't mean to hurt you right now, I need to assess the marital damage. You see, you may not have been aware of where your attachment with Allen has gone."

"Okay, what are the questions? I hope these are not trick questions, Raheem. I am in no mood for games. The Bible teaches us to guard our hearts and protect our love."

"Bea, are you talking to him about intimate aspects of our relationship? Things you are not talking about with me?"

Bea started playing with her wedding band, and answered, "Yes, but not much."

"Hold on, honey, I am not done," said Raheem. "Are you taking time and energy away from our relationship and giving it to your friendship with Allen? Are you two keeping secrets which I am not privy to?"

"Well, maybe, a few intimate things, but not much; not much."

" Well, does he know what's going on with you and in our marriage because I don't? I am begging for information you offer him freely. Bea, being a married woman and I am not judging, but, why are you not uncomfortable sharing these emotions and feelings with another man? All those things belong to me and me only."

Bea stood with her back against the rail, the ocean breeze blowing her hair gently back and forth, her mind racing, pouring over each question. "Well I—" She started a statement but did not finish.

" Wait, two more questions," Raheem continued. "Bea, are you more excited about your conversations with Allen than your conversations with me, your husband?"

"Raheem, I do talk to you, but you have been so busy. Allen makes time for me. Are you saying this is all my fault?" asked Bea.

"No, it is mostly mine, but I am saying I don't want another man standing in my spot. He needs to move, that is my spot. Bea, I am your husband. No one comes before me. I will not share one strand of hair on your head with another man."

He slipped his finger behind her ear to keep her hair back from her face. "Last question, Bea. Would you be uncomfortable if your husband was having this kind of relationship with another woman?"

Tears stung Bea's eyes. "I am guilty of all these questions. But I thought I was in control of my emotions. What do you want me to do?"

"Say goodbye to Allen. Never be alone with him again. He has crossed over the line and become a danger to our marriage. Drop him and run."

"Okay," Benita said. "I will talk to him tonight."

"No, no, no!" answered Raheem. "We will talk to him tonight."

"Raheem, , let me do it," said Benita.

"Alright, but you have to cut it off at the knees," said Raheem. "Bea, I know it seems so innocent in the beginning, but trust me, it can end up being more damaging to our relationship than a night of sexual affairs. For women, the most damaging affairs are ones where the connection is more emotional than sexual. Again, listen, Bea. One-time anonymous sexual encounters are the least difficult for couples to work through and heal from. Statistically, women have more trouble getting over an emotional connection than a man does with a lover. It may seem unfair, but it is true. Men have less trouble getting over the affair even if there was sex involved. We are not so connected to an emotional affair. The bottom line is we both should always seek to protect our hearts and minds from outside interference."

The dam Benita had erected in her heart broke, and she sobbed, "Okay, Raheem, let's talk. You are what is wrong with us. You take me for granted. I am afraid to be myself around you. I always feel as if I need to be perfect at all times. I wish you could go back to why we fell in love. You touched a need in me and made me feel safe. Now all I feel is afraid of losing you. The thought of you finding another woman's beauty and love more desirable than mine is unbearable. Based your love for me on the beauty of my soul and I know it will fade away with time. I am afraid your love for me will fade away as I age. Your love will disappear, like with my mom and dad."

Raheem took a deep breath. "Well, Bea I am here. I am trying. I do love looking into your beautiful face each day. Even more, I look forward to growing old with you, Mrs. Porter. I walked in on another man telling you how he feels about you. How do you think it makes me feel? How do you feel about him? Am I too late? Please tell me I am not too late to fight for our love. Benita, I've been working so hard these past two years I put you on the back burner. That was because you are my rock. But even rocks gleam in the sunlight. I am sorry."

"Raheem, you used to tell me the sun would never rise and set without you telling me you love me. You said my beauty would never fade in your eyes and we would always make time for each other. You said I would always be the most important thing in your life. You said those things, and now you don't remember how to keep your promises. You forgot about me. You used to send me flowers, chocolates, diamonds, weekend trips for 'you and me time.' Now you are gone all the time and when you are home you are still gone."

Raheem pulled her into his arms and held her close. "Benita, please forgive me. This has been a rough year for my hospital. With the Obama Healthcare bill, we have been so busy reorganizing and searching for the best

By: Willi Ray

healthcare plans for the entire company. I am sorry I let my career almost destroy our marriage. I did forget to tell you how important you are to me. Benita, without you, nothing works in my world. Bea, we need to talk about Mr. Allen."

Benita looked up at her six-foot-six husband. "Honey, I don't have feeling for Allen. I am in love with you, a man who treats me like I am invisible. I do not understand why men who ignore or cheat on their women are hurt to find out another man finds his reject desirable."

Raheem dropped his head. "No matter how busy a man gets building his kingdom, he doesn't ever want another man looking at or becoming emotionally attached to his queen. Lady, it was hard to stay composed when I saw Allen."

"Raheem I am not hard to look at, am I? When you don't do your homework, you leave me an open prey for other men."

Raheem kissed her lips gently. "Bea, let me say, you are everything I want in a woman. You are the most beautiful, gentle woman I know. You would never hurt a fly. You are almost perfect. Benita, no matter how long we live, you will always be the most beautiful woman in the world to me. The beauty I see when I look at you is the beauty of your face, your heart, your mind and soul. I promise to tell you how much I love and need and want you, Baby, every day. I may not always say it in words, but I will never leave you wondering about my love for you. I bought you a little something to say happy anniversary even though you forgot this time."

Benita's face lit up as she looked at the gift box he removed from his pocket. "What did you get me?" She reached for the well-decorated three-inch box.

"Open it and see."

"A necklace! It is so beautiful. It is a diamond necklace. Thank you, Baby."

"Yes, it is, but it does not compare to your beauty, Benita."

The other ladies had seen Raheem when he came out on the deck. Now they joined Raheem and Benita.

"Dr. Raheem." Sadie Mae hugged him. "It is so good to see a marriage that still works. How are you? I haven't seen you since Benita's last award appreciation dinner."

"Hey, Raheem," Lyneil said. "I did not know you were invited. It is so good to see you. You and Bea, keep your marriage strong. You two make a beautiful couple."

Dydbie added, "Yes, Raheem. Thanks for all your help. I don't know what I would do without you and Benita."

"You ladies are still our best friends. Thank all of you for standing by us. Now, if you ladies will excuse me, Ms. Bea and I have some unfinished business."

Benita took his hand. "Honey, one dance before we leave. There is a Tango contest coming up in a few minutes."

"Lead the way, Baby. It's been a long time since I danced with the most beautiful woman in the world."

Benita smiled and winked. "Romance is my weakness. I love a man who can charm the sweet fragrance off a rose. I am so hot for you right now."

"It will be my pleasure to accommodate you," Raheem breathed into her ear. "Tonight, it is all about you, me, and us. Let's Tango."

All the ladies and their partners danced the Tango. They were all putting their own sexy spin on it. It was like their swimsuit competition. They were all so competitive and loved celebrating their sisterhood and friendship.

After the dance, Benita said, "See you all tomorrow. Sadie Mae, I ordered you the suit, and we will discuss it tomorrow."

"Okay," Sadie Mae responded. "You two enjoy the night."

Later, when all the guests were leaving, the ladies talked about how wonderful their time in Jamaica had been.

"Luke," Dydbie said, "I will be in your area next month around the twenty-fifth. If you would like, we could get together for dinner. I will be in Japan tomorrow. Please keep in touch."

Luke hugged her and kissed her cheek. "I cannot wait to see you again, Ms. Dydbie. I will call you when I get to the airport."

By: Willi Ray

Paul said to Sadie Mae, "You are a lovely lady. I envy your husband. I also have to thank him for sending you to me twice. The third time he sends you I will not send you back. I feel like you are the missing piece to my happiness. Someone once said only a fool will allow himself to fall in love with another man's wife." He kissed her cheek and whispered in her ear, "Sadie Mae, I am almost gone."

Sadie Mae touched his face, her heart racing. Dydbie came and stood beside Sadie Mae. "I will walk you to the cab," she said.

"Thank you, girl," Sadie Mae said. "But to be clear," she whispered into Dydbie ear, "he is so fine."

Paul said, "Goodbye, Sadie Mae," and he walked away.

"Good night, ladies," Allen added. "Tell Benita I will call her next week to thank her for the invitation."

"I enjoyed the night," Kendal said. "I will see you again, I hope. Goodnight."

Lyneil said, "Kendal, if you like what you see say so."

"I would like to see you again," Kendal answered. "I move slowly because when I fall in love, I fall hard. You are the kind of woman I can lose myself in. Please allow me to peruse you on my own terms. I move slowly because I am checking for leaks, making plans for future dreams."

Lyneil laughed out loud, the kind of sexy, seductive laughter said, take your time. I am worth the wait. She leaned over as if she was going to kiss him, but as he closed his eyes and offered his lips, she stepped back and said, "Take your time."

Kendal opened his eyes and smiled. "I hope you use this time to cleanse your heart of your past and open your heart to something new. Safe Travels," Kendal said as he kissed her hand.

The ladies walked to their cab together. They all were feeling something they have not in years—alive.

Chapter 9

After her flight back from Jamaica, Sadie Mae took a cab home. She was happy her husband had not made it home yet. She went online and signed up for a weight management program. She saw it came with a health coach and she could lose three to five pounds a week. She only wanted to lose thirty pounds. The program meals would be delivered to her office in five days.

Later, a box arrived from Benita. A fat suit would make her look fifteen pounds heavier. She put it on and looked at herself in the mirror. Whoa! What a mess, she thought. She would never let herself get this big.

Good thing she would not be wearing this thing to work. Her confidence would be shot if she had to carry around all these additional pounds every day.

She hoped this would teach her husband a lesson he would never forget. It would either save her marriage or finish destroying it. If he didn't want her because she was fat, what would he do with this fat chick now? Well, let the games begin.

As she turned side to side, surveying her image in the mirror, the phone rang.

It was Benita. "Where is Michael? Did you put on the fat suit?"

"Yes, and it makes me look like I got fatter in three days. Benita, are you sure this will work?"

Benita laughed. "Well, Sadie Mae, since your marriage is not perfect, know this: It will not change your marriage for the better, but it may make him frustrated."

"Okay, I guess you are right. What do I have to lose? He doesn't love me anyway. Oh, Benita, I hear him coming now."

Michael entered the bedroom and both boys ran past him and hugged their mother.

Sadie Mae bent down to make eye contact with the boys and to hug and kiss them. "How are my two handsome men?"

"How was your trip?" Michael asked.

"It was great. Aren't you going to give me a hug and tell me you love me?" she taunted.

Michael looked Sadie Mae up and down. "The boys missed you, and I am hungry," he said without greeting her. "I assume you ate already. You look full," he growled and walked away.

"Well, cook yourself something," Sadie Mae called after him. "Most happily married women love cooking for their husbands. Too bad I don't fit that category."

"Most happily married men have beautiful, thin, shapely wives. Too bad you don't fit that category, and I am not happy about it. I see you came back fatter than before you left. I never thought you were the kind of woman who lets herself go like this. You look a hot mess."

Sadie Mae followed him. "Michael, you are a big hypocrite. You have gained forty pounds since we got married. I haven't mentally abused or rejected you. I've loved you unconditionally."

"I am a man and I carry my weight well. You don't."

"Is that why your six pack has turned into an old shack? Michael, man boobs are not appealing to women." She sighed and added, "Whatever. I missed you too, Sweetheart."

"Sadie Mae, go lose some weight!" Michael yelled.

"Don't fool yourself, Michael. To be clear, some men find me sexy."

Michael shook his head. "Sadie Mae, I don't want to fight with you tonight. I want you to give me back the person I married. Good night. I am sleeping in the guestroom. When my wife comes back, I will move back into our bedroom."

Sadie Mae stood there, speechless. She did not expect this. Tears welled up in her eyes and without a pause flooded her face. She could not bat them away fast enough. The front of her blouse soaked with tears within a few seconds. The pain ran through her heart was electrifying. It shocked her

By: Willi Ray

body and her soul. She couldn't help doubling over in agony as she watched the back of his head disappear around the corner. It was as if her feet were glued to the floor. She wanted to run catch him and slap the hell out of him and beg him to come to his senses, but the floor would not release her.

After a few minutes, life came back into her feet and the floor gave up her dead. She walked slowly into her bedroom and fell across the bed like a gunshot victim. She could not fight the urgency of her painful tears. She gave in and cried for two hours. Finally, she got up and took off the fat suit. No use wearing it anymore. He hated to look at her whether she was fifteen pounds heavier or not.

Eyes swollen and red from crying, Sadie Mae found the courage to force her lifeless body to rise when she heard small knocks on her bedroom door. Her motherly instinct took preference over her pain, and she left behind a pillow bearing witness to her emotional distress, soaked with tears and stained with mascara and lipstick. She opened the door. "I will make dinner for my two angels," she said. "How about Pizza and hot wings?"

"Yes!" the boys yelled and jumped up and down around her.

"Okay. We will make homemade pizza."

After the boys ate, she took them outside to ride their bikes. She sat in a lawn chair, chin in hand, watching them ride up and down the street. The wind gently swept over her hair and kissed her cheeks. She was so engrossed in her thoughts she did not notice new neighbors moving in four houses down.

Was this the end of her marriage, she wondered? Maybe she should lose weight to save her marriage. But if she lost weight to save the marriage, she was telling him it was okay to treat her like crap because she was not his ideal weight. Should she go through with the fat suit thing? She would not give in to his mental cruelty. She told herself, I am a person with real feelings and emotions. I deserve respect. I will teach this selfish, smug, vain, self-absorbed man a lesson if it is the last thing I do. Bring it on Michael. She stood up and called the boys to come to her.

"Boys, let's go in," she said. "It's bath time."

She filled the tub halfway with water and added half a cup of Dr. Teal's pure Epsom Salt Foaming Bubble Bath. "Come on in, guys. The bath is ready." The boys threw their clothes onto the floor and climbed into the bath tub. They were splashing around in no time, playing with their toys in the water.

Sadie Mae smiled, watching her two adorable sons. "I will be back in a few minutes," she told them. She walked down the hall toward the guestroom where her husband was sleeping. She put her hand on the knob, but something would not let her turn it to enter the room. Her heart would have forced her into the room out of fear of losing her marriage, but her mind weighed the impact it would have on her future happiness. She would never be free to exist in this marriage as a person if she entered the room tonight. He would always have the upper hand and become a coldhearted dictator. She couldn't allow it, and she backed away from the door.

She went into her bedroom and picked up the cell to call Benita.

"I need to talk," she said. "He hurt me today."

"What did he do," Benita asked, pausing her typing on the brief she had been working on.

Sadie Mae took a deep breath, choosing her words carefully. "He moved out of our bedroom. He said he would not move back in until his wife came back home. Benita, he is treating me like I am dead or like I killed his wife. What am I going to do?"

Benita sighed. "Well, Sadie Mae, let's talk about it. I have Lyn in my office. We are preparing for court tomorrow. She will be a free woman."

In the background, Lyn shouted out, "Freedom! Freedom! Yes, I have been waiting on the day to be rid of that tired jerk."

"I am so happy for you, Lyn," said Sadie Mae. "You deserve happiness and peace."

Benita butted back in. "Now, Sadie Mae, I am so sorry you are hurting. Do you want to promise him you are going to lose the weight in order to save the marriage? You can do it, if it is what you want. For centuries, women have been known to die for love. As Maya Angelou said, "A weak man cannot love a strong woman. He won't know what to do with her." So, you can die inside for this weak man or love yourself and live long enough to find a man strong enough to love you. I hope you lose the weight because you feel it will improve your health and not because you are pressured to do so by an ungrateful fool."

Lyneil laughed. "Sadie Mae, we can make him cry. Do you want us to make a plan of attack?"

By: Willi Ray

Sadie Mae paused. "I don't know yet. Since men are visual, do they have the right to ask women to fit the image in their fantasy, even if the fantasy is unrealistic? When will we learn most of the women who are shaped like Barbie dolls and are cut to perfection have their own share of problems? They are not real; they are manmade images of what men call their ideal woman. I am a real woman, with real curves and feeling. What gives a man the right to ask a woman to conform to these unrealistic images? The girls who are shaped like this and have not had surgery are teenage girls whose bodies have not fully developed yet. I have two boys and he is their father. I had not planned on being a single parent. Benita, I need to know if somewhere in his heart he still loves and wants us as a family. I have to believe deep down he loves me and the boys."

"Sadie Mae, I am a realist," Lyneil said. "And I believe we as women need to stop viewing life through rose-colored glasses. Give him a dose of his own medicine, and make it strong. If he loves you, as you believe, love will survive after you cure his ignorance."

Benita said, "Sadie Mae, why don't we test his love for you? If he fails, we teach him a lesson he will never forget."

"Okay, that will work for me," Sadie Mae said. "If he fails I will know my weight in not the problem and there is a bigger problem hiding behind my weight."

When she hung up the phone, Sadie Mae went back into the bathroom. "Boys, it is time to get out of the tub." She pulled two large towels from the shelf and dried the water from both boys' bodies. She lotion them down with Vaseline Intensive Care lotion, gently slipped their pajamas on and sent them both to their room. "I am on my way to tuck you in and help you with your prayers," she said.

Both boys got down on their knees beside their beds.

Michael Jr. began, "Our father which art in heaven, hollow would be thy name..."

Keith chimed in, "Thy kingdom come. There will be done..."

When they were done praying, they got into their beds and pulled up the comforters. "Can Daddy read us a story?" Keith asked.

"I will go ask him for you." She kissed them both and whispered, "I love you," to each of them and tucked the sheets tightly around them.

She went to the guestroom door. "Michael, the boys are waiting on you to read them a story."

"I am on my way," Michael said, and opened the door. He walked down the hall without making eye contact as he passed Sadie Mae.

"Let the war begin," Sadie Mae mumbled. "This is the end."

Michael stopped and looked back toward Sadie Mae, but all he saw was the closing of the bedroom door. The lock popped. He scratched his head with a puzzled look on his face. He had never felt such a cold wind blow like a blizzard coming his way.

Sitting on the side of the bed, reading *Jack in the Beanstalk*, Michael kept pausing. He could not help wondering what Sadie Mae meant when she said, "Let the war begin."

"Dad, why are you stopping so much?" Mike Jr. said. "Read the story."

"Yeah, Daddy," Keith added, read about Jack and the goose that laid the golden egg. Read it, Daddy, read it."

"Okay," Michael said. He started the story again, and when he looked up both boys were asleep. He put the book on the shelf, kissed the boys, and turned off the light.

He walked down the long hallway which seemed to have grown in length since the last time he walked down it. He stopped outside the master bedroom door to compose himself. So many apologies went through his mind. He failed to notice the feeling of the softness of the carpet between his toes because his entire body was one big ball of emotions. He was feeling so many things. He wanted to hold Sadie Mae and tell her how much he loved her. He was hoping it was not too late.

He knocked. No response. He knocked again. Still nothing but quiet from the bedroom. He couldn't have known Sadie Mae had taken two Tylenol PM capsules and gone to sleep.

"I love you, Sadie Mae," he whispered, walked away feeling rejected and ignored. He wondered if she still loved him or if her heart had moved on.

Back in the guestroom, he analyzed these thoughts. He was in the spotlight all the time, he told himself, he needed a woman who fit his lifestyle. He wanted his friends to see he was successful in every aspect of his life. He'd worked hard to achieve his dreams, and he needed a woman who looked like a dream. Why couldn't she lose the weight? He didn't understand her. She only needed to lose twenty-five pounds or so. She was beautiful, intelligent, and successful. He will make her lose the weight because he needed her on his team.

The Tylenol PM wore off at about 4:30 in the morning. Sadie Mae rolled over and looked at the pillow on the other side on the bed where Michael use to sleep. The moonlight was shining through the skylight in the ceiling. The bed looked bigger and colder than ever. She tossed and turned, trying to get back to sleep, but sleep would not come. She got up and walked to the window and gazed out at the quiet subdivision of Chicago.

Her life was changing before her eyes. Her mind went back to her wedding day. The way he looked at her, it was as if she was his treasure. The marriage vows he wrote were perfect. He promised to love her forever. But now she had gained a little weight, he couldn't love her at all.

She wondered, why some men lie so much? What was she going to do? She needed to keep her family together, but at what price? Why was her husband's love conditional? He could only love the girl he met in college; he couldn't love the woman she was today.

She turned on the television. *Law and Order* was coming on. It was an episode she had seen before; nevertheless, the noise was a welcome release from her thoughts. She lay in the bed watching the 90-inch Samsung television on the wall for about thirty minutes. *The Late Show* came on. She turned the channel to CNN and a conversation about Donald Trump calling Rosie O' Donnell a "Fat Pig" and labeling Miss Universe "Miss Piggy."

Those words cut her to her heart. She was angry that a man in the office of President of America had no respect for women. She was even more determined to make her husband change his views on women. She couldn't lay there any longer. She was hearing the influence of Donald Trump in her husband's voice. She looked at the clock as she searched with her toes for her house shoes on the floor beside the bed. Without looking down, her feet found the shoes and she slipped them on.

She stood up and walked over to the mirror. Gazing at her image, she took off all her clothes. She looked at her breasts, pushing up the right one, the left. They looked fine to her. What's not to love? She felt proud of her breast size. She turned to look at her hips and butt cheeks. A fully rounded apple bottom. What was his problem? She moved her hands up and down her hips. Was she too fat to love? She turned to view her body from every angle. Was she any less a human being than before; therefore, unlovable? She looked at her lips and cheeks. Had her kisses lost their sweetness? How had she become hideous to the man she married? She wished he would talk to her. His kind of love confused her.

Why couldn't she have it all—be a mother and still have the love of her husband? She elevated herself on her tiptoes. After all, she had earned it. She wanted peace with her body. New tears ran down her face and lapped under her chin. A few went into her mouth as she took a deep breath.

What she wanted was a marriage that worked and a man who loved her. What she wanted was for thick, fat, overweight, plump, and full-figured women to be in season. When was the right season to love a full-figured woman? What was the right time to gain weight? Did her husband think her being thin and shapely would eradicate all life's problems? Being thin did not guarantee happiness.

It is stupid for a man to buy into the American nightmare being thin makes you happy. Society and the advertising market would make you think the sun rose and set around skinny people. It was all a lie, people with a little weight on them were so miserable and some were suicidal. She loved the way she looked. But she would lose weight if he would show her he loved her. She sighed deeply.

She put her robe on again and went to the bathroom to take another round of Tylenol PM. When she returned to the bed, she turned on to her side and prayed to God. "Lord, if it is your will, can you save this marriage? Lord, he is my first love and the only man I've ever slept with. He is all I know. I grew up and matured into the woman I am today under the shadow of my husband. Maybe he has always been this way and I loved him so much I dismissed his actions. I was thin most of my life with him and maybe that is what he fell in love with. I lost the weight after my first pregnancy, but not the second. Maybe this is what has always been there and I have been blinded by my love. Why does love hide the true nature from the loving eyes seeking the truth?" She drifted off to sleep at 6:00AM,

By: Willi Ray

knowing she needed to be at work at 9:00AM.

It was Tuesday morning, two weeks after returning home from the Jamaica trip. Sadie Mae got up at 8:00AM. Everyone was gone. Michael dropped the boys off at school because it was on his way to work. Sadie Mae walked into her office and her day began. She was the top selling author on the label at her publishing company.

She had a 9:00 meeting with her editor and was working on the deadline for the release of her book *Broken*. She announced her book would be completed by the end of the year. The marketing department meeting was at 10:00 to pitch their presentation of the marketing strategies for the new book. The graphic designer and photographer were working on the book cover and putting the finishing touches on their work for their 11:30 meeting with the management team.

Sadie Mae planned to meet with her personal assistance before lunch to check her schedule and set up a meeting with the new artist on the label and talk show selections. She had a 1:30 meeting with the finance and advertising department to set the budget for the new book for the newly-signed artist.

"Am I done?" Sadie Mae asked Carol, her assistant. Carol was a thin, well-dressed professional woman with short blond hair. Sadie Mae always said she was pretty, but a little uptight and overdressed.

Carol placed a cup of coffee on the desk. "I left the 3:00 time slot open so you can go to Mike Jr.'s sax recital at 5:00."

"You are precious," Sadie Mae told Carol. "Thanks."

Carol laughed. "Remember me at Christmas," she joked.

Sadie Mae grabbed her black Prada purse and started to walk away. she turned back to Carol and asked, "Has Michael called today?"

"No," Carol said, "he has not called today, but I am sure he will."

Sadie Mae walked to the elevator. Where is the fat suit, she thought?

The UPS man was getting off the elevator as she was getting on. He had a box with her name on it. The label read, "Take Shape for Life."

"That is my food," Sadie Mae told him. "I guess I will be losing weight soon." She pushed the button for the first floor.

When she parked her white jaguar at the school and rushed into the building, she saw Michael going into the auditorium. "Hey, Mike," she called out, but he did not hear her. She stopped waving her hand in the air and calling his name. Okay, if that is the way he wanted to play this, he can have it his way.

Mike Jr. did a great job. When he finished, Sadie Mae stood up and shouted, "That's my baby," along with the audience's polite applause. When the program was over and the Principal dismissed the recital, Sadie Mae pushed her way through the crowd feeling so proud of her son. When she got up to the stage to congratulate Mike Jr., to her surprise, he was gone. How could Michael take him away before she had a chance to congratulate him? She rushed to her car and peeled out of the parking lot. In the privacy of her car, she screamed to the top of her voice. Her screams were put into words. "The low-down, dirty, sneaky man wants to play rough, let's roll."

When Sadie Mae got home, pulled into the garage, and barely closed the door to the kitchen, she yelled, "Michael, where are you?"

Mike Jr. came running around the corner. "Mom, why didn't you come to see me play tonight, Dad came ?"

Sadie Mae swallowed back her anger. "Honey, Mommy would never be in town and not come out to cheer for you. You are my gifted sax player. You did a wonderful job tonight."

"Mom, you did come? Dad said you were busy today, so he came."

"Honey, I love you, and I am never too busy for you."

Sadie Mae hugged Mike Jr. and said, "Your dad must have misunderstood me. I promise you I will clear this up with your father."

Keith came into the kitchen. "Mommy, Dad said he will be back later. Can I have some cereal, please?"

"Wait a minute, Keith."

Sadie Mae ran to the garage. Michael's 700 series black BMW was pulling out of the driveway and the garage door was going down. She whispered, "Sometimes I hate that man!"

Keith overheard his mother. "Mommy, was Daddy bad today? Do you hate him?" Keith looked up at his mother; his head tilted back, his curly hair lying gently against his forehead. He squished his little blue eyes closed as he waited on an answer from him mother. He had eyelashes most women would kill to have, long and curved up on the ends.

Sadie Mae was so frustrated with Michael, but she put it aside. "Okay, little man. Mommy is sorry. Now what is for dinner? How about making some pancakes and sausages?"

"Mom, you rock!" replied Keith.

Mike Jr. added, "Yeah. Cool!"

The boys went to do their homework, and while she started cooking, Sadie Mae called Michael. "Why did you tell our son I was too busy to come to his recital? How could you be so mean?"

Michael sarcastic asked, "Sadie, have you lost any weight yet?"

Sadie Mae shouted back, "Michael, have you grown a brain yet?"

"Do not call me again," Michael said, "until you lose some weight. I did not want to be seen with you in public. I have an image to keep, Fat Girl. Get off my phone and go lose some weight. I am not going to keep begging you to put this marriage back together. If you want this marriage, lose the weight," he shouted at the top of his voice. "What I decide to tell my sons about you in not your problem. Your problem is you being big and fat. Solve it!"

Sadie Mae could not imagine a more freezing conversation, but the argument had already escalated to new heights. "You are so stupid, you self-absorbed nitwit," she shouted. "I gave you two sons and you treat me like this? You need to find a place to stay. I will not have you disrespecting me and turning my children against me. The locks will be changed whenever you decide to come back. Your clothes with be in the trash can out back." She hung up.

She grabbed her chest, thinking she must be having a panic attack. How could he be so cruel? When did he turn into this monster? She was breathing heavily and trying to stay in control but the physical pain in her chest and the emotional pain from her broken heart were overpowering her efforts to stay in control. She started shaking and crying from the pressure.

It was all hitting her so hard—the realization he did not want the marriage, and he did not love her anymore. Her hands shook so much she could not get the spatula under the pancakes to flip them. The sausages were starting to burn and the tears falling in the skillet popped and spattered. Smoke started to fill the kitchen and the smoke detector went off. The noise of the smoke detector drowned out the sound of her sobs.

Mike Jr. came running into the kitchen. "Mom, Mom, there is so much smoke in here. Mom! Did you burn yourself? Why are you crying?"

Sadie Mae did not answer. She gave in to her pain of her crying.

Mike Jr. was so afraid he called his dad. He shouted, "Dad, Dad, Mom is crying. Please come home."

Michael felt mixed emotions. "Son, she will be okay. I will check on her later. She is having a bad day. I got to go."

"But Dad," Mike Jr. said, "the house is on fire! Come home."

Michael had music in his car blasting, so he did not hear the last thing Mike Jr. said. "Son, take care of your mom." And he hung up. He was so angry because Sadie Mae told him to find another place to stay; his pride would not let him go back to see what was wrong with Sadie Mae.

Mike Jr. called Benita. "Aunt Benita," he said, "Mom is crying and the house is filled with smoke. The smoke detector is going off. The pancakes are brunt and the sausages are smoking badly. Dad won't come home. Can you help Mom?"

"Go over to the stove and turn it off," Benita instructed. "Now let me speak to your mom."

"The stove is off and Mom is fanning the smoke detector," he said. "There is so much smoke, and she is crying. Mom, Aunt Benita is on the phone."

"Baby, did you call Aunt Benita?"

"Yes, Mom. I called Aunt Benita because you need some help. I called Dad and he wouldn't come home. Mom, what is wrong?"

Sadie Mae took the phone and put it to her ear, still talking to Mike Jr.

By: Willi Ray

"Honey, you called your dad, and he would not come home?"

"Yes, Mom. He told me to take care of you, so I called Aunt Benita. I am only six and I did not know what to do." He started crying. "Mom, what is wrong? Why won't Dad come home and why are you crying and burning up the house? Mom, what's wrong?" he cried.

Sadie Mae put down the phone and hugged Mike Jr. "Everything is going to be alright. I am sick, and the smoke got in my eyes and that's why I am crying."

Benita yelled into the phone. "Sadie Mae, Sadie Mae!" but no one answered. She hung up the phone and called and Dydbie and Lyneil. "Ladies, Sadie Mae is breaking down. She needs us. Can you all work out of Chicago? We need to be near and help with the boys."

Dydbie asked, "Where is her husband?"

"Little Michael said he won't come home," Benita replied.

"My next project isn't until next month," Dydbie said. "I will be there tomorrow morning."

"Okay, and I will leave right after court tomorrow," Benita added. "This is the final divorce proceeding for Lyneil."

Lyneil said, "I am so worried about Sadie Mae, I don't know if I am going to be able to celebrate my divorce. Bea, I will be there in two weeks. I may have to finish working on a solution to tailor our business and guarantee the most pressing problems get solved. It will evaluate trial performance and proactively manage risks using industry standards and metrics. It will "Crosswalk" our internal and external data to unlock valuable business insights."

Benita said okay, Lyneil you are making progress in the new company cash cow. Thank you all for clearing your schedules and they hung up.

Sadie Mae went to check on Keith. He had slept through the entire crisis in the kitchen.

"Mike, honey, do you want Chinese food? I am ordering now," said

Broken

Sadie Mae.

Mike screamed excitedly, "Yes, Mom. I will have sweet and sour chicken. Keith likes ham fried rice. Can I have your fortune cookie, Mom? You never eat yours."

"Yes, honey. Now let me check your homework while we wait on the Chinese food."

Forty-five minutes later the doorbell rang. The food had arrived. Sadie Mae woke Keith and told him to come into the kitchen for dinner.

Keith stood and stretched. "Are the pancakes ready?"

Sadie Mae stroked his curly hair. "No, Baby, we are not having pancakes. We are having Chinese food."

Keith started crying. "But I don't want Chinese food, I want pancakes, Mom. You said we were having pancakes. Where are my pancakes, Mom?" He cried for five minutes.

Sadie Mae took a deep breath, realizing her children were also feeling the stress of the marital issues. She wanted to let everything go and run to her room and close the door, but she realized she needed to be a calming force. She wiped her forehead, took a deep breath, took her son into her arms and held him, rubbing his back and consoling him with kisses. "It's okay, Honey. Sometimes we do not get everything we want."

Mike Jr. kept right on eating through the screaming. His fork never missed his mouth. "Keith, shut up, man. Eat your rice," he said.

"No! I want pancakes, Bighead!" He kept on crying.

"Don't call your brother names, Keith, Baby," Sadie Mae whispered. "Please stop crying." She walked around the kitchen, holding him in her arms, until he stopped crying. She sat down at the table and took a fork to feed him as she sang and rocked him. She spoon-fed him until he had had enough to eat. She kissed him on the cheek and asked if he was ready for his bubble bath.

Looking up at his mom with his big, wide eyes, he said, "Yes, Mommy. My duck needs a bath too. Mommy, I am not a big baby. I'm sorry."

Mike Jr. shouted, "Yes, you are a big cry baby. But we still love you."

By: Willi Ray

Sadie Mae was so happy he stopped crying. She ran a bath with a million bubbles in it.

As the boys splashed around in the water, she sat by the bathtub. She was struggling to find the right words to tell the boys their father would not be living with them anymore. "Hey, guys, Daddy will be on a business trip for a while, so we need to take care of each other." She picked up the washcloth and started bathing the boys. "I am going to work harder to be a better mommy," she said as she helped them out of the tub and wiped them dry. She wrapped a big fluffy white towel around each of them. After rubbing them down with lotion, she asked if they wanted to hear a song or a story.

"Yes, a song, Mom," said Mike. Can you sing "A Beautiful Surprise" by India Arie?

Sadie Mae smiled. "Wow, your taste in music has matured. Daddy bought me the CD and I like her music. Okay, Mike Jr., I need to listen to it to make sure it's safe for your age."

Keith, jumping around in his jammies, said, "No, Mommy, sing Michael Jackson, "Thriller." I am Michael Jackson, Mommy. Mom, sit down and watch this."

"Yeah, Mom, he has been practicing for weeks to surprise you," said Mike Jr.

Keith jumped up and put a white glove on his left hand and rolled his pants legs up. He ran and got one of his daddy's hats. He looked like a mini Michael Jackson. He put his "Thriller" soundtrack in. When the song started to play, he never missed a beat. He even moon walked across the room.

Sadie Mae laughed and clapped her hands. "Honey, you are wonderful! She picked him up and placed him in her lap. she sang "A Beautiful Surprise." When she was done, both boys were fast asleep. She kissed them, tucked them in, and turned off the light.

She went into her bedroom and grabbed Michael's suits, shoes, and other personal things and stuffed them into six trash bags. She placed the bags on the back patio. Sweaty and tired, she sat down to gather her thoughts. She told herself, today is the last time I cry because of Michael Crenshaw. Tomorrow I will be stronger than ever before. I will fight back with everything I have inside of me.

She picked up the phone to call Benita. "I am so sorry, Benita. My life is a mess right now. I put Michael out today because he was belittling me and turning my children against me. Benita, I don't understand men. Why would he give up on us after seven years?"

"Are you okay, Sadie Mae? I am concerned about you."

"Benita, my world stopped. I held out hope these past few months' believing things would work themselves out. I am disappointed and heartbroken."

"Were the kids and the pressure too much for you tonight?" asked Benita. "Can you call your mother for support?"

"No, I don't want to worry my mother. She hates Michael. She does not have an objective opinion about him," said Sadie Mae, "and my father needs one more reason to beat him down. We both lost our family support when we married outside our own race. It was me and him against the world," said Sadie Mae.

"But your father gave you away," said Benita.

"Yes, he did, but he was not happy about giving his only daughter to a white man. Dad kept his promise to pay for the wedding and not to interfere. So, he stays away."

"I am so sorry," said Benita. "I never knew. Sadie Mae, I don't know how objective I can be," Benita added. "I am overly concerned about your mental state right now. You should not be alone—"

"Hold on, Benita," Sadie Mae interrupted, "someone is at the door. I hope it is not Michael because I will hurt him right now."

Chapter 10

"Guess who!" Dydbie surprised Sadie Mae when she opened the door. "Benita said you needed help, and I came right away."

"Benita, it's Dydbie at the door," Sadie Mae said into the phone.

"She got there fast," said Benita.

Dydbie smiled. "Sadie Mae, how are you doing? I am here as long as you need me. You don't have to be alone. We are here for you. Those frequent flier miles come in handy in a crunch."

"Dyd got there in three hours!" Benita's voice was filled with relief. "Sadie Mae, I won't have to worry now. You are in good hands. I will be there next week. Love you." She hung up the phone.

Sadie Mae and Dydbie talked and laughed half the night. "I am so glad you are here, Dydbie. I felt stressed and emotional. Michael is my life; I can't believe he doesn't think about me."

"Give it some time," Dydbie said. "I am sure he thinks about you. You are his wife and the mother of his children."

"It hurts so bad, Dydbie."

"Why don't you get some sleep? I won't let him hurt you anymore. In the morning I will get the kids dressed, fed, and off to school. You go take a hot shower. I got this."

She hugged Sadie Mae. "Now where do I sleep?"

"You are the fourth room on the left." Sadie Mae pointed down the hall. "Dydbie, God knew I needed you tonight. I burned the dinner, smoked up the house, and cried into the sausage pan. It has been a rough day, and my son saw me have a meltdown."

"I am here," said Dydbie. "We are stronger together."

"Good night, Dydbie, and thank you for coming."

Sadie Mae took two Tylenol PM and was out for the night, or, so she thought.

Later, the phone rang. Dydbie picked up the receiver. "Sadie Mae, are you okay?" It was Michael. "I tried to act like I do not care, but you know I do. lose the weight, okay?"

"I am sorry, Sir," Dydbie said. "You have the wrong number." She hung up.

Michael held the phone in his hand with the dial tone humming. "Sadie, don't do this," he whispered.

Sadie Mae opened her door. "Who was on the phone?"

"Wrong number," Dydbie answered.

Sadie Mae walked into the family room. I will make us some tea so we can talk. I forgot to tell you I need to change the linens on your bed in the guestroom.

Dydbie looked at Sadie Mae with concern. "Yes, I am glad I am here with you, Sadie Mae. You only slept an hour and here you are back up again. Didn't you take Tylenol PM?"

"Yes, and my head does feel funny," said Sadie Mae, "but the phone call woke me up. I need a friend right now. You have always been so thin and beautiful, you couldn't possibly know how it feels to have the man you love strip you of your dignity. It hurts so bad. I trusted him to love me for better or for worse. How could I have been so wrong about Michael?"

Dydbie walked over and sat down by Sadie Mae. "Girl, you are not fat. Full-figured women are a big market now. Sadie Mae, real talk. The reason I came to your side so fast is because I do understand. Sadie Mae, I was beaten four years during a five-year marriage. My self-esteem was so low, and getting lower. Blow after blow, he took me a little lower until I had no more self-esteem in me. I lived in fear. The worst pain was dealing with the Post Traumatic Stress Syndrome. Even when he is not beating me, the reoccurring nightmare of the prior beating would not let me sleep. Every time a man touched me I almost jumped out of my skin. I hated myself and the situation I was in. But the verbal abuse you are living with is as bad as the physical abuse I lived with. They both leave scars and destroy self-esteem. As an abused woman, I did not seek help. For years, I denied there was a problem. Verbal abuse is another form of fighting, with words or language. The Bible said words are a two-edged sword, cutting going and coming. An abusive man can do as much damage with words as he can with his fists. Most unhappy men project their own insecurity and self-hatred onto their wives. They hit us because they don't like the man in the mirror. They feel powerless to make positive change."

"That's right, Dydbie," Sadie Mae said. "I never thought of it that way. And I know so many women who are abused, but I never thought of myself as one of them. We must educate women on recognizing abuse, weather verbal or physical. Well, I am looking at being a single mother raising two young sons. Dydbie, this is my life, and someone else is making all the decisions. I did not choose this. I don't want to fight this kind of battle, but now the fight is on." She was quiet for a moment, whispered, "What do I do with all this love I have in my heart for him? How do you fight someone you love so much?"

"Let me tell you how I survived," Dydbie said. "I kept on breathing, one breath at a time, even when everything within me wanted to die. I prayed a lot and God let you guys come to my rescue when I needed you most. If you guys had not helped me when you did, he would have killed me. The beatings were getting more and more severe. I did not think my body could survive another beating. So, because of where I've been in my life, I can help you get through the tough time now. Sadie Mae, you can lean on me, we have a sisterhood only death can separate. I don't think you are fat. I think you are hot, girl."

"Thank you, Dydbie. You are a true friend. You have proven to be the exception to the bubble-headed model theory." She laughed. "I love you girl, this is a true example of female bonding. You are my girl! You know what to say. I never want to be one of those women who give love so easy, without drama, without a price tag, and without a back-door plan. Men walk on that type of women who come bearing only love. All I have to offer is love. I don't have time for drama."

"A good man will see what you have to offer as an asset."

"Let me get your room ready," Sadie Mae said. "Everything you need is here. I'll get up at 6:00 to get the children ready. I don't have to be at work until eight tomorrow."

The Tylenol PM was working now. Sadie Mae could barely get to her room.

"Don't you worry about a thing," Dydbie said. "Let me help you get into bed. I think you are going to get some sleep tonight."

The next morning Dydbie was up making coffee when Sadie Mae walked into the kitchen. "You look picture perfect," said Sadie Mae. "You do know I don't have photographers to snap your picture, right." She laughed.

Dyd laughed. "LOL, Sadie Mae. I'll take the children to school for you. It will give us a chance to bond. I have not seen them in a year. I brought gifts for them too. What would you like for dinner?"

"Don't kill my boys," Sadie Mae laughed with her. "Whatever you cook will be fine. I do have a housekeeper who comes in four days a week. She cooks and cleans. She is off Friday, Saturday, and Sunday. She is in by 9:00 AM and out by 4:00 PM. Her name is Sue. You will like her. She is nice."

After a sip of coffee, Sadie Mae added, "Dydbie, do you still want that large family you talked about so much in college?"

Dydbie's face lit up, and she sat a little straighter. You could hear the smile in her voice as she said, "I do. But it was never the right time." the smile went out of her face. "When the beatings started I was relieved I did not have any children to witness the abuse. If I find the right man I want to settle down and have two boys and two girls. Sadie Mae, you are blessed to have children."

"They are my greatest inspiration," Sadie Mae said. "I never thought I would find so much joy in motherhood. Now, if I can fix this marriage—"

"Well, God is in control," Dydbie said. "I hope he comes to his senses." They both laughed.

"What do you think about Luke?" Dydbie asked. "He is so cute, and he is a good catch, but I am afraid of getting into a relationship this early."

Sadie Mae saw the concern and fear on Dydbie's face. She wanted to encourage her and tell her to take a chance on Luke, but she understood it might be too soon. "Luke is handsome, and crazy about you," was all she said.

Chapter 11

Benita and Lyneil showed up in court for the divorce hearing. Lynn looked across the way at her husband, who was still wearing smug look on his face. He stared straight ahead. His lawyer leaned in to whisper in his ear.

Everyone stood at the demand of the bailiff's voice in the half-empty room as the judge entered the courtroom. Her long black robe and long serious face adorned with glasses on her nose reminded Lyneil of the Quaker Oaks man. Was she a by-the-book kind of judge, thought Lyneil? Lyneil found it amusing this judge would soon change the stupid smile on her soon-to-be-ex-husband.

Everyone sat down again, and the judge called for the attorneys to approach the bench. After a few minutes of low conversation, the attorneys returned to their seats.

Lyneil's husband, Steve Gazella, turned and smiled, making kissing gestures at her as his lawyer stood to speak. "Your Honor, we respectfully ask that you throw out the alienation of affection charges. This is unfounded. There is no factual evidence of my client being unfaithful. This divorce should be granted on irreconcilable differences. We will present a case of desertion and abandonment by the wife. Mrs. Gazella moved out of town without notifying her husband."

"I object, your honor!" Benita stood. "We will prove Mr. Gazella was an unfaithful husband, and was mentally and emotionally abusive to his wife."

Mr. Gazelle's attorney's name was Brownstone, and he came highly recommended. He had never lost a case, and he was paid big bucks to get down and dirty. He only represented men in divorce proceedings.

"Your honor," Attorney Brownstone continued smoothly, "we were not informed of any evidence against my client."

Looking down her nose, the judge said, "Counselors, meet me in my chambers. We need to talk."

When they reconvened in the judge's chambers, she asked, "What evidence do you have to prove Mr. Gazella was unfaithful to his wife?"

Benita answered, "Your honor, we have pictures with dates, times, and places where Mr. Gazella met with his lover during his marriage."

"This is highly prejudicial against my client," Brownstone charged. "We are just now becoming aware there are pictures and a tracking log of his alleged comings and goings. We need the name of the witness and time to review this material."

The judge looked at the pictures. "I will allow the pictures. I hope your client can explain these bedroom shots."

"Your honor," Brownstone continued, "this man's reputation is at stake."

"Council," the judge addressed Benita, "can you prove your case of infidelity without these nude bedroom pictures?"

Wanting to embarrass and humiliate Mr. Gazella as he had done to his wife, she answered, "Your Honor, we do have financial records of the gifts he purchased for his lover out of the martial finances. We also have proof his lover was stalking my client. My client spoke to her husband about it. He did nothing to protect my client, so she was forced to move to another state out of fear for her life."

The judge sighed. "Attorney Porter, I will allow the photos as long as you have sufficient grounds to support your case."

The divorce proceedings began.

Benita called Cindy Wynhaven to the stand. Mr. Gazella dropped his head, looked over at Lyneil with a look that could kill. Lyneil took a piece of tissue from her purse and dabbed the corners of her eyes, smiled at him.

Cindy turned another shade of pink as she was being sworn in with the Bible.

"Please state your full name for the court," Benita ordered.

"My name is Cindy Renee Wynhaven."

"Ms. Wynhaven, are you having an affair with Mr. Gazella?"

"No!" Cindy shouted. "No, I am not. I only know him from work."

By: Willi Ray

"Lower your voice, please, Ms. Wynhaven. Listen to the question again. Are you sure you are not having an affair with Mr. Gazella?"

"We are friends."

"Did you know your friend was married?"

"No."

"Have you ever met his wife?"

"No."

Benita walked to her table and grabbed an envelope. Mr. Gazella's lips got tight, and he looked away. "Ms. Wynhaven, please look at these pictures and tell the court who these people are in the pictures and what they are doing."

Cindy took the pictures. The shock at seeing her and her lover in bed having sex with the window open was written all over her face. "Oh, my God!" she shouted. "I plead the Fifth Amendment!" she started to weep.

"Answer the question, please," said the judge, "or you will be held in contempt of court."

"The people in the pictures are me and Mr. Gazella," Cindy whimpered. "I did not know he was married."

"Ms. Wynhaven, on the night on March 15, on a Tuesday at about 6:00PM, you called Mr. Gazella and his wife answered the phone. Do you remember that conversation?"

"Yes," Cindy whispered. "She said she was his wife, but she could have been lying. I told her I was calling because my son was looking for his father."

"Do you have a child?"

"No, but—"

"Ms. Wynhaven, the car you drive: Who financed the car and who makes the payments?"

Suddenly bold, Cindy boasted, "Mr. Gazella pays for it. And I am his woman. He doesn't love her. He loves me. We want to be together."

"Do you have respect for the institution of marriage?" Benita asked. "Is this the first time you have met Mrs. Gazella?"

"Yes, I have respect for marriage, but it is not my fault he wants me. Some men like something more than plain sex and boring meals with a simple woman. I've never met his wife, other than talking to her on the phone one night."

"Look at the video screen, please. Do you recognize these two people talking at the mall?"

"What?" Cindy shouted. "Yes, it's me and his wife. But I have a right to privacy and you all have interrupted my life."

"How many other times have you stalked Mrs. Gazella?" Benita added, "And before you answer, be warned I have—"

Brownstone jumped up and shouted, "Objection, Your Honor."

The judge looked down her long nose and slowly parted her nearly invisible lips. "Please rephrase the question."

Benita walked away, turned and asked, "How many times have you and Mrs. Gazella been in the same place at the same time?"

"I don't know, and I don't care," cried Cindy. "She works too much, and she is never around to take care of his needs."

"And you are?" asked Benita.

"He told me she was too busy for him, and he needed a woman who knows how to please a man. I believe a woman should walk behind her man and not in front. She should follow him and not lead. She won't let him be a man. I need a good man and I got him," said Cindy.

"Yes, you do," replied Benita. "You should look up the word good, Ms. Wynhaven. I have no more questions for this witness."

Brownstone approached the witness stand. "Ms. Wynhaven, did you set out to date a married man?"

"No. His wife was always working, and he was left to fend for himself. So, we kept meeting up at the same restaurant."

By: Willi Ray

"No more questions for this witness."

Next, Brownstone said, "The court calls Mr. Gazella to the stand."

After Mr. Gazella had been sworn in, Mr. Brownstone asked, "Over the last year, how often was your wife out of town or working late?"

"She was home about three nights out of seven. I got lonely, and I was tired of being the last one on her list. She let that company go to her head, and she stopped being a wife."

"Objection, Your Honor," Benita called. "Women are allowed to work. This is America, and many couples have worked out their careers and marriages without infidelity or cheating."

"Sustained," the judge stated.

Brownstone changed his line of questioning. "How did you find out your wife had moved out of state?"

"She stopped coming home, and I got a change of address letter in the mail. I was so hurt she did not talk to me about this. I love my wife, but she is in love with power."

"No more questions. Your witness."

Benita stood, smiled, and said, "Good morning, Mr. Gazella. Did you have a good night's sleep last night?"

"Your Honor," Brownstone whined, "I object. My client's sleeping habits have no bearing on the case today."

"Attorney Porter, where are you going with this line of questioning?" the judge asked.

"I have a few questions on where and with whom he has been sleeping, but I will redirect the question. Mr. Gazella, when did your affair with Ms. Wynhaven begin?"

"About three months ago. And I did not plan this."

"Of course, you didn't. The car you purchased for Ms. Wynhaven was financed in January 2013. So, do you make it a habit to buy cars for complete strangers?"

"No, that car was bought by my company. Ms. Wynhaven did not get the car until July, after her car broke down."

"Did you check the address on the license plate registration for the car? Can you read for the court the date of the plates and the address they were registered to?"

Mr. Gazelle became irritated. "January 2013, and the Address is 3245 Parkway Avenue, Apartment B, Columbia, South Carolina."

"So, did you make a mistake or are you lying about whom the car was purchased for? Do you know how many lies you and Ms. Wynhaven have told this court?"

Brownstone shouted, "Objection. Counsel is badgering the witness."

"I will allow it," the judge sang out. "Answer the question."

Mr. Gazella's face looked uncomfortable and his voice took on a sarcastic edge. "When I walked in here and saw a female judge and a female attorney, I knew I would not get a fair trial. This chicken coop is full of dried up old hens good for nothing but dropping in a pot of boiling water for dinner."

Benita shouted, "Your Honor—" But before she could finish her statement, the judge slammed her gavel down, hitting three sharp blows on the block, and stating, "One more disrespectful remark, Mr. Gazella, and I will hold you in contempt of court. Attorney Brownstone, control your client." The judge was now awake and taking even more dislike to Mr. Gazella than before.

Embarrassed by his client's outburst, Attorney Brownstone asked, "May I have a moment to speak to my client, Your Honor?"

"Don't talk to me about anything," Gazella blustered. "I am going to speak my mind. I am going to pay for it anyway. My wife doesn't need a husband, she has a PhD in business, and she is the VP of a big Fortune 500 company. Hell, she is one step from being a lesbian. She does not need a man. You women need to learn men are the head of the marriage and your job is to help men achieve their goals and be the breadwinner. Men should not have to compete with their wives for the power and authority in a marriage. I don't think women should be running multi-million-dollar companies. She should be at home having babies and cooking and cleaning the house. That's the kind of wife I need. Now how much is it going to cost me to get out of this non-functional institution called marriage?" He pointed at Lyneil. "She is what the

By: Willi Ray

Bible calls an ostrich. She buries her head in the sand when the storm comes, and she doesn't have enough common sense to care for her household. Good riddance! She didn't help me build up my company because she was running around making money for everyone else."

The judge slammed the gavel again and shouted, "Order in the court! I have heard enough. The divorce is granted on the condition Mrs. Gazella specified—alienation of affection. Marital property valued at 1.8 million is awarded to Mr. Gazella. Bank and savings accounts totaling 3.7 million, split 80/40—eighty percent in favor of Mrs. Gazella. Stocks and bonds, split 70/40—seventy percent in favor of Mrs. Gazella. Mr. Gazella, you will retain your company and all its assets. Mr. Gazella will pay Mrs. Gazella $275,000 for infidelity during the marriage, court costs, and attorney fees. Mrs. Gazella is granted her maiden name, Rubentol."

"I don't have that kind of money," Mr. Gazella shouted. "She is not worth $275,000. Sex wasn't that good to pay her that kind of money. It would have been cheaper to keep the witch. I knew you women would side with her because of the gender thing. Attorney Brownstone, say something. I am paying you big money and you are letting her railroad me. You are fired, I want my money back. Get out of my face."

The judge slammed her gavel on the desk, shouting, "Order in the court! Mr. Gazella, if I have to warn you again, you will spend three nights in jail for contempt of court and pay a fine of $50,000."

"There is no justice in this divorce," he shouted. "Attorney, open your mouth and defend me! Say something!"

Attorney Brownstone looked at Mr. Gazella and shook his head. "I did say something, when I asked you to stop talking, but you said all the wrong things to a woman judge. Please be quiet before she has you jailed for a year."

"Ms. Wynhaven," the judge instructed, "you should have had an attorney present."

In a disagreeable tone, Cindy replied, "I don't need an attorney. It is not a crime to sleep with a married man. The way I see it, it's her loss, my gain."

The judge continued, "Ms. Wynhaven, you are out on bail for a prostitution charge. So, If I were you, I would shut my mouth. Have you ever heard of the term Criminal Conversion?"

In a humbler attitude, Cindy said, "Your Honor, I am not a prostitute, and I am not a criminal, so none of that applies to me."

"The court fines Ms. Wynhaven $150,000 for Criminal Conversion or one year in jail. Ms. Wynhaven, in the future, do your fornicating outside of this state."

Cindy's blond hair swept around her head as she shook it vehemently. "She won't get a penny from me. What does that mean? I am not paying that woman any money. She broke up her own marriage. I slept with her husband; I did not break up their marriage. It's not my fault he doesn't want to be with her. I have to pay her for being stupid enough to send me her husband gift wrapped with a bow? No way!"

"Mr. Gazella, I can see why she fits your outdated views on marriage and women. She is as dumb as they come, and a prostitute, too. Mr. Gazella, I am sure your mother would be proud of you. $175,000 is the new amount, Ms. Wynhaven, and it is to be paid within twelve months by both parties."

"Ms. Rubentol, do you feel you need a restraining order against these two?"

"No, Your Honor," Lyneil replied, "as long as they are both instructed to discontinue all communication with me as of today."

"Mr. Gazella and Ms. Wynhaven, are you in agreement with discontinuing all communication with Ms. Rubentol right now?"

"Yes, I agree," Cindy answered. "I should have whipped her butt when I saw her in the mall. Now I won't get a chance."

Lyneil said, "Your Honor, I change my mind. I do need one against Ms. Wynhaven. I would hate to pop a hole in her hot air balloon."

"Granted."

"Thank you, Your Honor," Lyneil said.

Mr. Gazella said, "Cindy, you open your mouth one more time, and I am going to—" He stopped suddenly. "I will abide by the rules of the court."

"Ms. Wynhaven," the judge added, "you need to reconsider your choice in men."

By: Willi Ray

Benita concluded, "Thank you, Your Honor."

Mr. Gazella looked at Lyneil as she passed him and winked. The police were approaching him with handcuffs for his three days in jail.

After the free-for-all, Lyneil thanked Benita, and asked, "How did you get all that evidence?"

"I have my ways. Besides, you ladies are my family and I will do whatever I need to do to protect you as you would me. It's all good for the sisterhood. How shall we celebrate?"

"Let's go to church and shout, 'Thank you, Jesus!' I am free at last."

"I say let's call Sadie Mae and Dydbie from the limo, Ms. Rubentol."

Lyneil dialed Sadie Mae's number. "Hey, Sadie Mae, is Dydbie with you? I have great news."

"Yes, she's here," Sadie Mae replied. "I'll put you on speakerphone. Dydbie, come quick. Lyneil and Benita are on the phone."

Dydbie asked, "How did court go?"

"It was beautiful," Lyneil said. "You should have seen Benita. She was better than Perry Mason. The girl is bad. I am glad she was on my side. My ex-husband and his girlfriend both are paying top dollar for the price of their sins."

"So," Sadie Mae laughed, "what did Benita say her major was under that law degree?"

"Making grown men cry," answered Benita, "and paying for their evil doings."

"Yes, thank you, Jesus!" Lyneil added.

"So, Lyn, you are a single lady again. How does it feel to be free?"

"Happy, sad. Good and bad. I don't know yet. I feel like I did when I first got out of college, excited and empty."

"Now, make arrangements to celebrate Lyneil's freedom with us, Sadie Mae," Benita said. "I have rooms at the Hilton Hotel tomorrow night.

Can you meet us there?"

Sadie Mae answered, "I know the place. See you tomorrow. I will make all the arrangements and I've got the wardrobe covered as well."

Chapter 12

Sadie Mae's phone rang. "Hello?" she answered. No response on the other end. She hung up.

The phone rang again. This time Dydbie answered. Michael said, "Sadie Mae, I am sorry about not coming back to check on you when Mike Jr. called. What are we doing?"

"Michael, this is Dydbie. Hold on. I will get Sadie Mae."

"Why are you in my house?" Michael asked. "Is Sadie Mae sick? What's going on?"

"With all your bad behavior and bad treatment of your wife, Michael! I am here to help Sadie Mae. Whatever problems you two are having, I hope you can work them out."

"We can fix our problems without anyone else interfering. Stay out of my way. Sadie Mae needs to lose the weight."

"You almost fooled me," Dydbie said. "I was about to get Sadie Mae to the phone, but not for this type of stupid behavior. That woman loves you and all she wants is to keep her family together. I used to admire and respect you. I was the maid of honor at your wedding. I never knew you were a creep and a womanizer. Abuse I know all too well. Whether it's physical or verbal, it still has the same effects. How could you turn her life into a nightmare?"

"This is none of your business. I love my family and my wife. I need her thirty pounds thinner. I cannot believe all this confusion is because she refuses to lose the weight. I would like it if things got back to the way they were before she gained all the weight. Why can some women keep it together and others turn into a chunky donkey? Having a baby is no excuse for being fat. I am a man and I need to be successful in my marriage and my career path. I want it all and I will not apologize for wanting a wife that fits into my world."

Sadie Mae saw Dydbie talking on the phone. She walked over and took the phone in time to hear Michael say, "Having a baby is no excuse to be fat…" Her heart dropped.

"Michael, why are you so mean?" Sadie Mae yelled. "You will reap what you sow. I hate you, Michael Crenshaw, to be clear, Michael, go to hell!" She hung up the phone, went into her room, and closed the door.

As the tears fell, there was a knock at the door. Dydbie kept knocking. "Sadie Mae, are you okay? Can I come in? Honey, I know you are in there."

Sadie Mae wiped her eyes and opened the door. "Come in, Dydbie. I am sorry. But Michael can be so cruel. How can I love a man who treats me so bad, Dydbie? Sometime I wish the bruises were physical because I could see the scar as it heals, but these invisible scars are too hard to bear. They have a ripening effect going from my heart, soul, and body. It cuts like a knife over and over again. There are no pain medications that can stop this kind of pain. Sometimes the pain takes my breath away. I did not prepare well for this kind of problem. I have so many things running through my mind, but I am not confused or disillusioned."

Dydbie wrapped her arms around her friend. "I know how hard it is to bear."

"If I give in to this kind of pressure what's the next thing he will bully me into? He and I have so many deeply rooted differences within our racial makeup. We should be standing together to fight hate and bigotry, waging an internal war because one of us does not fit into what society defines as successful. I cannot give in to his wishes because my sons are black and at what point will they not fit into my husband's perfect world? Dydbie, it is not about fitting into the ill views of society, but tolerance and acceptance."

Dydbie saw the hurt and pain all over Sadie Mae's face. "I am so sorry, but it will get easier soon. Okay, this is much bigger than the weight gain. You are trying to get him to see the scope of bigotry and how he will have to continue to sacrifice to this ugly demonic force. I know bigotry is a demon with a big appetite and I can't help you. Benita will be here tomorrow. She will help you get this under control. Benita always knows what to do. I am here for you, but unfortunately I am not as resourceful as Benita."

Sadie Mae hugged Dydbie and said, "Your being here has given me the strength I need to stand up and be strong for my children and to fight for my right to be happy in whatever stage my body and life finds me in. I cannot express my thanks to you for dropping everything and coming to help me as a friend and a powerful ally."

By: Willi Ray

"Honey, during these hard times we learn what we are made of, and I am betting you are stronger than you know. The Bible says weeping shall endure for a night, but joy comes in the morning. Sadie Mae, if I were not a Christian, I could not have made it through this nightmare I've lived through with my husband. I am a believer. You can do all things through Christ who loves you. Now how about some tea to help you sleep?"

"So, you are a Christian too?"

"Yes, and it hasn't always been easy. Sadie Mae, I am going to share this with you." She paused to choose her words. "I had told myself I was going to take this to my grave.

"What is it, girl?" Sadie Mae looked serious. "Do I need to sit down?"

"Yes," said Dydbie. "When I was being beaten by my husband, I went to my Pastor and told him and asked for help. Yes, I was black and blue at the time to prove the truth. I was told, 'Your husband is head of the household and I cannot interfere in your marriage unless he asks for help.' I was told to have him come and talk to the church and ask for help."

"Why would he ask for help?" Sadie Mae asked. "He was not the one being beaten. In his mind, everything was under control. Being head of the household meant he could keep beating you because it was his God-given right."

"I went to the church mother," Dydbie continued. "She said, 'You made your bed, now lay in it.' The church is not always a safe haven for abused women. The church needs training and resources to help women. I called the police twice, and they could not do anything, because, as they said, 'Your husband is a powerful man. Don't make trouble.' The one time I was pregnant, he beat the baby out of me."

"Did he know you were pregnant?" Sadie Mae said, "Can I quote from *The Color Purple*? 'I will kill Harpo dead before I let him beat me.' Why didn't you kill him?"

"No, he did not know I was pregnant. I was now afraid for two people instead of one. I did not want my unborn child to be born into that kind of hell. I was so depressed. When I lost the baby—forgive me for saying this—I was relieved the baby died."

"Dyd, I am so sorry. I love you, my tower of faith."

"Sadie Mae, please do not tell the other ladies. Now where is the tea?"

Sadie Mae smiled and wiped her eyes. "It will be our secret forever. I got some raspberry sleepy time tea. I will show you where it is. I am organized so don't mess up my system." They both laughed.

"I remember the sock drawer trick," Dydbie said. "Do you remember when Benita mixed up your socks and panties drawer? You had a fit when your sock drawer was messed up. The funniest thing was Benita hid one of the matches to every sock you owned. You tore our two-bedroom apartment apart looking for those socks. The funny part was, all your socks were black so what difference did it make they were not the original mates?"

"I knew," Sadie Mae asserted. "It did not matter what anyone else thought. I knew those socks were mismatched. I like order."

They drank their tea and talked until they got sleepy.

Next morning, Dydbie got up and made the children pancakes. She turned on the television to get the weather and news before waking the children. Sadie Mae smelled the coffee. After she got out of the shower, she put on her robe and found her way to the kitchen.

"Good morning, Sadie Mae," Dydbie greeted her cheerfully. "How did you sleep?"

"I slept good and reminiscing about our college days. Thanks for making me laugh last night. I pray this will be a great day."

"Well, Sadie Mae, whatever the day brings you can handle it because you are blessed and highly favored."

"Can I be honest with you, Dydbie?"

"Of course, what is it?"

"I am so angry with God right now. I trusted him to keep my marriage together. He turned a deaf ear to my prayer. I needed him and he was not there. Where was God when I needed him most? How can he allow things to get this bad? When is he going to do something?" As she spoke her eye welled up with tears and her lip quivered.

By: Willi Ray

"Sadie Mae, if you need someone to blame, go ahead and blame God. He can handle it. Take out your frustrations on him. He can take it. But Sadie Mae, the truth is, God had nothing to do with the falling apart from our marriages. He outlined the road map and blueprint to a good successful marriage right there in the pages of the Bible. It takes two to keep a marriage together. Sadie Mae, after you are done blaming God, you have to forgive Him and let it go. You are going to have to forgive your Michael too, but that will come in time. Let's work on God first. If you keep all that anger and hatred inside it will hurt you more than you can imagine. Come here, baby. Go ahead and cry. Get it all out. I am your sister and I am not going anywhere. When you hurt I hurt, and when you smile my world is a little brighter"

"No, Dydbie. I will not cry anymore. I am so tired of crying." Tears rolled down her face as she kept repeating, "I am not going to cry, Dydbie. I won't cry. No! No!"

"Honey, you are already crying. Stop fighting it. Let it go."

Sadie Mae laid her head on Dydbie's shoulder and Dydbie's arms embraced her and gently rubbed her back. "It is going to get easier and you will get stronger. I promise."

"I asked God what I did wrong to get this type of man. He said, 'Your standards were too low.' He did not earn me. I was young and so happy a man with money wanted me, so I made it easy for him. God told me my value was higher than gold and rubies, but I never knew the value of my womanhood. No one ever taught me I was a self-contained treasure for the right man."

Dydbie continued to rub Sadie Mae's back as she spoke.

"If I had made him earn me, he would have treated me much better than those expensive cars he has on scheduled upkeep and car washes to stand and admire from a distance. He feels powerful when he is riding in his expensive cars because he had to earn them. They cost him something, so they have value to him."

the doorbell rang.

"I will get it," Dydbie said. "I am already dressed."

"If is Michael," Sadie Mae sniffled, "tell him to go to hell!"

"I will get rid of him." She walked to the door and snatched it open.

"What do you want, Michael?" she screamed. "Hey, it's about time you all got here."

In the kitchen, Sadie Mae was sure it was Michael. She ran to the bathroom and started putting on lipstick and checking her face. She was so hoping it was Michael. She wanted to look good while yelling at her husband. She was angry with him, but she loved him more than she hated him. So many emotions ran through her heart. Though her eyes were bloodshot and her nose red from crying, she returned to the kitchen waiting with anticipation for Michael to find her. Her heart beat fast and her face was warm. Her mind searched for the right words to say. Her eyes dared to blink in hope that he was coming home. She held her breath. She could barely stand still as the sound of footsteps on the hardwood floor grew closer. Around the corner appeared Benita and Lyneil with Dydbie.

"Hello," Benita said.

Before the word was out of Benita's mouth, Sadie Mae burst into hysterical crying. Her eyes looked even bigger when they were filled with tears. Sadie Mae was so disappointed it was not Michael, and at the same time, so happy to see her girls. She ran to her room, fell upon her bed, and sobbed.

"What did I say?" asked Benita. "Wow! I have never seen Sadie Mae so upset."

"It was your face, Benita," teased Lyneil. "You scared her like you did those men in the courtroom."

Lyneil removed her off-white Gucci jacket and red Gucci Boston handbag and laid them on the arm of the couch before following Sadie Mae. "Sadie Mae, honey, we are here for you."

Dydbie placed her Bentley Platinum sunglasses and orange Hermes Birkin Himalayan Niloticus Crocodile purse on the table.

"This is serious, Benita," Dydbie said. "I don't know what else to do. She cries all the time. Can you help her?"

"I am not God," Benita responded, "but I will do what I can," placing her Black Dolce Gabbana DG20273 sunglasses and her Marc Jacobs Carolyn Croc Handbag on the table. Benita took a deep breath as she walked into Sadie Mae's bedroom. "Honey, what's wrong, neat freak? Your room is a total mess."

"Don't mention God," Dydbie whispered, "because she is mad at him right now."

"What did God do?" Lyneil asked.

"She blames him for the marriage falling apart. I'll make some more coffee; we may be here all day."

Benita stroked Sadie Mae's hair. "Honey, sit up. We need to talk."

"Can we talk tomorrow?" Sadie Mae moaned. "I feel sick."

Benita came back to the family room. "Well, she put me out."

Lyneil suggested, "Do we need to pray with her first?"

"How can we do that when she is mad at God?" Dydbie asked.

"Nonsense!" stated Lyneil. "God did not tell her to marry that crazy man."

The ladies sat facing the hallway to Sadie Mae's room, discussing their trip and anticipating her coming out to talk, but the morning faded to noon and noon to night. Sadie Mae stayed in her room all day, hurt, embarrassed and confused.

"You all got any plans?" Dydbie asked as they sat waiting for Sadie Mae to come out.

"Well, tomorrow may be a better day to assess the damages and a plan of correction," Benita said.

"Good luck," said Dydbie. "I am going to bed. I got all cute today and didn't even leave the house. Wow! Not like me."

Everyone retired to the guestrooms for the night.

The next morning, the doorbell rang. "Who is it?" Lyneil asked when she answered it.

She returned to the kitchen. "It's a little boy from down the street, looking for Mike Jr. He asked if Mike Jr. was going to school."

"Oh, my goodness!" Dydbie said. "I forgot to get the boys up for school."

"What time does the bus come?" asked Benita.

"7:00 or 8:00, I think."

Benita laughed. "Dyd, how long have you been here? You've gotten the boys up for school the last three days this week. How did you forget about them?"

Dydbie said, "I will get the children up and ready for school. They are so cute. You've got to see them."

"Dydbie, you get them bathed. I will get their clothes and their breakfast ready," Benita said.

Lyneil said, "I brought them the cutest outfits from Macy's. I'll get them."

Benita made oatmeal and poured juice and packed lunches. Dydbie bathed and dried the children and lotion them down.

Lyneil said, "Good morning, my babies!"

They ran to her shouting, "Aunt Lyneil!"

Lyneil knelt down to make eye contact and hug both boys. "How are my two handsome men doing? You two are even more handsome than the last time I saw you. I bought you two some new toys and a video game." She dressed both boys in blue jeans and white shirts with red and white baseball caps. "You two look wonderful," she said and kissed them again.

"Breakfast is ready," Benita called.

Both boys hugged Benita's legs. She bent down to hug and kiss them.

Benita stood in the kitchen smiling, her hair pulled back into a ponytail and no makeup. She looked like a teenager. Her freckles were visible. "You boys want to eat?"

"Yeah!" they shouted.

"This is almost as good as Daddy's oatmeal," Keith said. "Where is my mommy and daddy?"

By: Willi Ray

"Daddy is working and Mom is getting ready," said Benita. "Mommy will be out in a few minutes."

Mike Jr. looked at Benita and stated, "I am not a baby. I know Dad wants a divorce because Mom is fat. So, he left home because he hates all of us."

Lyneil's heart went out to Michael Jr. "Honey, remember what we talked about? Mom and Dad have grownup problems, and they separated for a little while, so they could talk about it later. Mike, do not mention the word fat again or your mom will murder you."

"Wow, Lyn, you don't want to scare the child," laughed Benita, kissing Mike Jr. on the check.

"Mike, please do not talk about this in front of your brother," Dydbie said. "We will talk about it later. Now let's go give your mom a hug."

"Okay," said Mike Jr., "but you all better talk because he is not blind, and Daddy has moved out. He is a smart kid."

Dydbie went into the bedroom and Sadie Mae was laying across the bed looking out the window. "Honey, the children are ready to leave for the bus. Are you getting up?"

"Yes, Lyn," Sadie Mae said. "I was thinking, look at this beautiful day God gave me today in spite of all the confusion in my life. This is God's way to saying it will all work out. I trust God will fix this thing. I am not going to fight this battle because God has heard my prayers and seen my tears. Now where are my two strong men?" She called out as she got up and started down the hall.

"I am in the kitchen, Mom," Mike answered, "having a grownup talk with Aunt Lyn."

Sadie Mae came into the kitchen laughing. She hugged both boys and kissed them. "Good morning, my little darlings."

Dydbie said, "Hey, the bus is coming."

"I am taking you boys skating after school," Benita said as she gave them their turkey sandwiches bagged for lunch.

"Come on, boys," Sadie Mae said. "I will walk you to the bus stop." She walked outside and the bus was picking up all the children on the block. Sadie Mae bent down to kiss the boys and whisper I love you. As she balanced herself in preparation to stand up, she noticed a pair of size 11 black Stacey Adams shoes. The pants were black and neatly covered the tops of the shoes. As she scanned up, she saw a crisp starched white, French-cuffed shirt with gold-plated diamond cufflinks, and the smell of cologne filled the air. The smell of him made her heart skip a beat. She loved a good-smelling man. For a second, she missed him, then her anger took over. She rose slowly to her feet as the voice announced, "I am taking the boys to school today."

"Michael, the boys can ride the bus. Please leave now."

The boys were jumping around, yelling, "Daddy, Daddy!" He picked them both up and walked to his BMW.

Sadie Mae was on fire, but she knew she had to remain calm because of the boys. "Have a good day, boys," she called out, while gasping for air.

She told herself she hated him. But the truth was, those few seconds of seeing him renewed the strong feelings she had for him.

"So much for taking the boys skating," Benita said to herself. "We have a bigger problem."

Chapter 13.

Benita had been standing outside and saw how disrespectfully Michael treated Sadie Mae. "Michael, I need to teach you some manners," she whispered.

Sadie Mae trudged up the steps to the house. "Give me a minute," she said. "I am going to cancel my meeting today.

Michael texted Sadie Mae. "I will come there and take care of the boys while you hang out with those three witches."

Sadie Mae was starting to get her strength back, her fight and quick-witted was back. She called Michael on the phone. Michael you do not get to disrespect my friends. Don't push me, Michael.

Michael slammed down the phone. He had a plan. He had bought some weight-loss pills and, he needed to get into the house to plant them where Sadie Mae would take them without suspecting anything. He was determined to make her lose weight.

"Sadie Mae, did you make a reservation to celebrate Lyn's divorce with us?" Benita asked.

"Yes. We have reservations at Fleming's Steakhouse at 7:00 tonight. The Windy City Limousine will be here at 6:00. Do you all want to go to a comedy or a Jazz show?"

"Where is Fleming's Steakhouse located?" asked Dydbie.

"On the corner of Ohio and Wabash, 25 East Ohio Street."

"What are we wearing tonight?" Lyneil asked.

"Niemen Marcus will be here at 4:00 with a rack of suits and dresses. I gave them your sizes and your favorite colors," Sadie Mae said.

The Niemen Marcus truck pulled up and rolled out a rack of clothes. The ladies tried on different things and picked out their favorite outfits. Sadie Mae paid the bill. As Niemen Marcus left, Sadie Mae's beautician arrived with his hands full of stuff. He came in and set up and within an hour and a half all four heads were done. They all went to their rooms to dress.

Sadie Mae looked stunning in her off-white pantsuit and sky-blue halter which was sheer around the waist and lace at the top. As she checked her makeup in the mirror, the door opened and in walked Michael.

Sadie Mae stood there owning the room. She looked at Michael, barely making eye contact. "I am asking you to knock on the door when you come over," she said coolly. "Your key will not work here soon and there will be a sign hanging on the front door saying you don't live here anymore. Your key only works here when your heart is softened. Don't make me change the locks," said Sadie Mae as she walked past him.

"I live here too," Michael said. "I don't want to fight. I haven't seen you looking so beautiful in a long time. You look amazing. Think of how much more beautiful you could be if you lose that extra weight. Your eyes; I've never seen a more beautiful set of eyes. It looks like you have lost some weight. Wow, you are hot."

Sadie Mae stopped and made eye contact. "Cut the crap, Michael. To be clear, the woman you married is dead. Now you have to deal with me, the woman you don't want. I promise you may not love me, but you will respect me. Now get out of my bedroom."

"You need to calm yourself down, Heart," Michael said. "I am only trying to compliment you."

"You haven't called me 'Heart' since your youngest son was born. Go to Hell, Michael, and take that pompous male attitude with you!" The fact is when he called her 'Heart' brought back old feeling, and she was back down memory lane.

Benita walked in and stood next to Sadie Mae. "How are you, Michael?"

Michael acknowledged her. "Benita."

By: Willi Ray

Dydbie said, "Hello, Michael. We are here for Sadie Mae and the children, and you, Michael, should not want to upset three witches!"

"Good to see all of you," Michael lied. "I hope we can keep this thing clean around my boys. Where are my children? I don't want them picking up bad habits from three witches."

"Why, Michael," Benita said, "what would make you think we would be anything but nice witches to the boys?"

Dydbie walked over and looked Michael in the face. "Let's be real, stupid. Witch is not our names, simple boy. You need to show some respect. We would not be here if you were being a husband and a real man. You yellow-bellied Pimp. You better remember whenever Sadie Mae cries, we three witches get overly-protective. And you don't want four angry witches sticking pins in a doll."

Benita walked up to him and whispered, "I would hate to mess up your stupid smile doing an attitude adjustment on you."

Lyneil smiled. "I do so hope you keep this thing nice. I would hate to use hocus-pocus to grow you a brain on the side of that long nose of yours, being a witch and all."

The kids came running into the room.

"How are my little men?" Michael said. "How about we go get pizza and make it a movie night? Give me a minute, guys. I have to use the bathroom."

He went into the master suite bathroom. He whispered, "I got some Brazilian diets pills for you, my chunky princess. Let's see who wins the weight-loss fight. Where are those One-A-Day Vitamins? Got it!" He poured the vitamin tablets down the toilet, refilled the bottle with the diet pills then returned to the room where the children were waiting.

"Goodnight, ladies. Don't eat too much. Those girlish figures could suffer a setback." He laughed and walked out, singing, "I ain't gonna bump no more with no big fat woman."

"Michael," Benita called after him, "you did not learn how to play nice in the sandbox at school. Maybe that explains why you feel you can bully your wife. You and I are going to become really close friends, very, very soon."

"Don't forget whose house this is," said Michael. "I may have to get my 'witch-be-gone' spray to get rid of you."

Sadie Mae said, "Michael, when you bring the boys back, we should talk."

"Anything you say, Princess Chunky."

The limo was waiting to take the ladies to dinner.

As they rode, Sadie Mae said, "I am so sorry you all witnessed him being a complete jerk."

"That's putting it nicely," Lyneil said. I don't think I can turn this ship around because this ship is sailing so fast and it is out of control.

I can't believe my marriage is on the rocks. I've tried so hard to make this thing work. I pray for Michael night and day that he would look at the shipwreck we will make and turn this thing around. It takes two parents to raise well-adjusted children. Why is he doing this to me? Why is he bent on destroying our family? Why does the man I love hate me so much? What have I done but love him and give him two sons?"

She continued, "Benita, I don't know if I can live without him. He is my first in everything. He is the only man I've slept with, the only man I have ever loved. I trusted him with my heart, my love, and my soul. I don't know what I can do to save this marriage."

"Let's change the subject," Dydbie said. "Sadie Mae, stop upsetting yourself. We will discuss it tomorrow and help you work through your feelings. Breathe and wipe your eyes."

"Baby girl, we all understand how you feel," Lyneil said. "Now he gave you an ultimatum—lose the weight, and he will love you again and give you back your life. The choice is yours, Sadie. We women sacrifice everything, including our souls for the love of a man. What is your price, Sadie Mae?"

"I don't know what my price is," Sadie Mae answered. "All I know is, love used to be free. I have been paying for love with blood, sweat, and tears. The price is too high. But I am not sure if I won't pay any price to save my marriage."

By: Willi Ray

"The choice is yours," Benita said. "Tomorrow we will put our heads together and analyze your life, hopes, and dreams. Maybe we can inspire your fight one way or the other. You know we are here to support you in whatever choice you make."

"I'm free!" Lyneil shouted. "Give us free!"

Dydbie said, "There was a powerful, patient man who put pen to paper and wrote these words: 'It's been a long time coming but a change is gonna come.' Sing the song for me, Sadie Mae."

Lyneil added, "Sadie Mae, my musical muse, bring this song to life. But while you are singing, could you keep your clothes on? No more shrinking dresses." They all laughed.

"And you almost came up missing," Dydbie said.

"You are one to talk," Benita said. "The shrinking dresses were your idea."

"I am amazed your ex-husband was not the butt of some of your cruel jokes," Sadie Mae said.

"Why are you smiling?" Dydbie asked. "Tell it!"

Lyneil laughed. "I took my new ex-husband's favorite Omega Cartier watch to the jeweler and had 'Male Whore' engraved in Italian on the face. He thanked me."

"Did you tell him what it meant?" Benita asked.

"No, it was my private joke every time he got dressed for work."

"Was that the only joke, Lyneil?" Sadie Mae laughed. "To be clear, we know you like playing jokes."

"It was a private joke," Lyneil laughed. "When he told me the woman who was calling his phone was his single male friend's girl, I put her number on Facebook with a message to call for a free lap dance. I also posted his number on a gay man dating site."

"Well, that is one of those little things I will take to my grave," Benita chuckled.

"I'll bet that was the best one," Dydbie said.

"I will say he couldn't sit down for a week, and he had to work from home for three days," Lyneil confided.

Sadie Mae joked, "Tell me Exlax was not involved."

Lyneil said, "Okay, back to the shrinking dresses. Where was I? Oh, yes, sorry for dredging up bad memories. I almost died that night. Sadie Mae, there will never be another wardrobe malfunction coming from me. Now ladies tonight, say party! Party over here, party! Party over there. Oah, oah, oah! Michael better look out because you look good, girl. Did you see the man over there watching you today?"

"Okay, Lyn, you are changing the subject. You are not going to tell us."

"Lyn, this is your night, and we will celebrate," said Dydbie. "Girl, you deserve a party."

After about forty-five minutes, the limo pulled up to the restaurant. They went in and ordered their food.

"I would like to make a toast," Benita said, "to the second time around, it can be sweet. A toast to being young, single, and free. What a winning hand."

All their glasses floated into the air and each word said was filled with encouragement and joy for Lyneil.

After dinner, they stepped outside to wait on the limo. The cold brisk Chicago air was a painful type of cold, the kind that separated the morrow and the bone. They climbed into the car and went to a concert hall.

"Earth Wind and Fire are playing tonight," Sadie Mae said.

"The Elements," quipped Lyneil. "I love them."

They sat and talked while the musicians hypnotized the room with their smooth jazz sounds. Sadie Mae was asked to sing *Change Is Gonna Come*. After the band did three more songs the night ended with Earth Wind and Fire's final song. The ladies gathered themselves and climbed into the limo again.

By: Willi Ray

On the way home, Sadie Mae said, "Tell me you all saw the 2016 Republican National Convention. Melania Trump repeated Michelle Obama's speech word for word. After I got past the weird accent, I said what's wrong with her she has no self-respect? Now she will be known as the person who hijacked Michelle's speech."

Benita laughed for a long time. "It was embarrassing to see a First Lady plagiarize another First Lady. I was speechless. But I laughed until it hurt because Trump's slogan is "Make America Great Again." Both of them come off as incompetent.

"Well, you know America is in trouble when the First Lady can't write a speech and steals a recent First Lady's speech," Lyneil added. "It would have been better if she had stolen Jackie Kennedy's speech. She has a speech impediment and Melania has a choking kind of accent, which makes English sound like another language."

"That night I could not say a word," Dydbie said. "I was utterly shocked she thought no one would remember those were Michelle's words. I turned the TV off after that because it was so sad."

Lyneil said, "Enough about the Trumps. I want to thank all of you for celebrating with me. Sadie Mae, none of this would be possible without my three favorite friends. My life is so much richer because of you all."

Benita was busy checking her messages.

"You all took my mind off my issues," said Sadie Mae. "I've enjoyed myself."

When they arrived at Sadie Mae's house, Michael was there with the boys. He put them to bed and he was asleep on the couch. Benita and Lyneil went on to their suites at the Union Station. Dydbie walked in with Sadie Mae, saw Michael on the couch, and went on to her room.

"Good night, Sadie Mae," she whispered. "I will leave my door cracked in case you need me."

Several weeks later, Sadie Mae got up one morning, made her a shake, took her vitamin, and climbed into the shower. She shampooed her hair and let the water run over her head and down the curve of her back. She thought about her day. She had a 9:30 meeting with the marketing team, and there was an 11:00 meeting with the new employees. She would meet Benita and the girls for lunch to confirm Dydbie's appearance with the Oprah Winfrey Show, finish the day with a 4:00 financial meeting with her CFO.

A troubling wave of nausea swept through her. The food she had last night did not agree with her. She hoped her stomach would settle soon because she had a lot to do today. She stepped out of the shower and grabbed one of the big six-foot-long pink towels from the shelf in the bathroom. She weighed herself. Whoa! She had lost another six pounds.

Reaching for the hair dryer and setting gel, she thought how she couldn't believe it was December already. Christmas was around the corner, and she had not gotten the boys' gifts yet. She picked up the phone to call Michael; remembered things were so different now.

Michael must be going through a mid-life crisis. And besides, he didn't love her anymore. "He doesn't love me anymore," she whispered as she wiped the steam from the mirror. She took a deep breath. The thought of living without Michael sent excruciating pain through her body. It stung and made her heart palpitate. "No," she told herself. "I am going to survive, and today is the first day of survival mode."

She put the finishing touches on her makeup. Her lipstick was the last thing she put on. She applied her pink lipstick, and took a tissue and patted away the excess. She picked up her Ralph Lauren Ricky purse and went to the kitchen. Her stomach still a little weak. She hoped it would wear off in a couple hours.

Dydbie and the children were having breakfast.

"Good morning, Dydbie. What's on your agenda today?" she asked.

"I have a 10:00 meeting in St. Louis, and I will be back by 1:00," Dydbie answered. "I will not be able to have lunch with you all, unless you can move lunch to 1:00. I got the kids. I'll drop them off at school by 8:00 and go on to the airport."

"I've lost six pounds," Sadie Mae told her. "I feel a little weak this morning, but I am sure I will feel better as my day goes on. Hopefully, I will see you all at lunch."

By: Willi Ray

"That's great! But I have to ask, are you losing it because you want to or because of all the undue pressure coming from Michael?"

"For me, I think. I am under so much pressure until I don't know anymore. I want my life back." She grabbed her briefcase and opened the garage door to get into her car.

When the morning was over, Sadie Mae headed to the Olive Garden to meet the ladies. Benita and Lyneil were there waiting in the lounge. They saw Sadie Mae pull up and park her car, and right behind her, like a whirlwind came Dydbie in a red BMW sports car.

Over lunch, Sadie Mae told the ladies, "You are my greatest inspiration. You all moved in and have been here sixty days, taking care of me and my boys. Thank you, ladies. You mean everything to me." They hugged as if they were seeing each other after a long absence, and they all shouted, "Sisterhood!"

Sadie Mae took out her vitamin bottle and took another one to give her more strength. Benita noticed the bottle Sadie Mae took from her purse.

"Sadie Mae, are those One-A-Day Vitamins helping?"

"I don't know, but I would feel worse without them.

"I would not have believed the way Michael treats you like a disobedient redheaded step-child," Lyneil commented. "His attitude needs some adjustment. What happened to the wonderful, gentle white man you married? He is horrible now. As long as the two of you have been married, I've never seen him as a white man before this. It felt as if you were not fighting within a marriage, but fighting a battle of race and sex."

"Come on, Lyneil," said Dydbie. "He has never called her the N-word, though he did call her names. Mixed couples can fight without race being part of the fight. I was the maid of honor at your wedding. There was no black or white, just two people in love."

"Well now," Lyneil said, "it's weird because all I see lately is a man being mean to the mother of his children."

"No matter how angry and disappointed he is in me now," Sadie Mae said, "I know deep down he still loves me. We are going through a tough time right now. I can't believe I said it, but what else am I supposed to say? He is my husband."

Benita said, "Keep it together, Sadie Mae. Find the courage to stand up and be strong. Michael was brutal and disrespectful, but why is he so angry? What are the two of you really fighting over? It has to be more than a little weight gain. Is there another woman he is comparing you to?"

"No!" Sadie Mae answered. "As far as I know, it is all about the weight gain. All his friends have these skinny trophy wives, and he is a successful businessman and as he has repeatedly said, he needs a wife that fits into his agenda."

"So, do you think the problem is because you gained weight you have lost your sex appeal with him and the blinders came off?" Benita asked. "Therefore, he sees you as an ordinary black woman?"

Sadie Mae's eyes got bigger. "Are you saying in his eyes I can't be sexy and over weight? Being beautiful and sexy hides the fact that I am a black woman? Because I am overweight he sees me as a color and not his wife? No, Michael is my husband. He is not like that."

"Sadie Mae, be careful that you do not run into the wall Michael has built between you and him," Benita warned. "My question is, why has he not divorced you if you do not fit into his agenda?"

Sadie Mae was obviously irritated by Benita's question. "I like to think it is because he still loves me."

"Maybe," Lyneil said, "but I am with Benita. There is a missing piece here. Why not divorce you and go find a trophy wife to impress his friends?"

Feeling and sensing Sadie Mae's body language, Dydbie said, "Sadie Mae, let us know if we need to change the subject. I know how hard it is to discuss the pieces of your life with your friends. Only the two of you truly know what is going on."

"Yes, it is painful to talk about my life as if my marriage is over. I have to hold out hope. I know you all mean well, but I am starting to feel like I am being judged on both sides of this thing."

Chapter 14

Benita concluded, "With that being said, let's change the subject. For the support of the sisterhood, just know we are here until you feel strong enough to decide, and we will support you no matter what you decide, no judgement."

After lunch, Sadie Mae went back to work with a lot to think about.

Two weeks went by and Sadie Mae lost five more pounds. She felt sicker by the day. She assumed the vitamins should help her feel better, but she kept feeling worse.

Sadie Mae lay on the couch between running back and forth to the bathroom to throw up. Dydbie was concerned. "Sadie Mae, it's great you are losing weight, but I think you need to see a doctor."

"Okay," Sadie Mae moaned. "I tried to make an appointment, but they can't get me in to see the doctor until next week. My head hurts something terrible. I can't keep any food on my stomach. I am nauseated and dizzy.

"Maybe it is all this stress of fighting with Michael," Lyneil suggested. "You two have been at this for four months."

"This feels different," Sadie Mae said. "If I wasn't sure, I couldn't be, I would think I am pregnant. I have a meeting at 10:00. I need to get up. I think I am coming down with the flu. If I get some rest, maybe I'll feel better."

Benita showed up at Michael's office at 4:00. A young woman with short brunette hair sat behind the desk. Her hair was tapered on both sides and the full-frontal cut flowed across her forehead. She looked to be about twenty-two years old.

"I have an appointment to see Michael Crenshaw," Benita told her.

The receptionist buzzed Michael's intercom. "Attorney Porter is here to see you."

"I do not have a meeting with whoever that is," Michael answered. "I am on my way to the gym. Get rid of her."

Benita overheard Michael. She walked past the receptionist, who had hung up the phone. "You can't go in there!" the young lady shouted.

"Go home or sit this one out," Benita responded over her shoulder.

Benita forced the door open to Michael's office. "You may not like what I have to say, but you are damn well going to listen."

"Come in, Attorney Porter," Michael said sarcastically. "Imagine an attorney being arrested for breaking and entering."

Benita walked straight to Michael's desk. "You have no idea who I am and what I am capable of," she responded. Benita was dressed in a navy-blue skirt suite with white and navy blue four and a half inch pumps. Her skirt was two inches over her knees, showing off her long, muscular legs."

"You are a skinny little blond-haired, blue-eyed white woman at about 120 pounds. Oh, yeah, I am shaking in my boots," he laughed.

Benita sat down, crossed her long, shapely legs, and removed her sunglasses. "My first approach is a peaceful one so go ahead and gets your giggles. Now, why do you want Sadie Mae to lose weight so bad, bad enough to walk out on your marriage and those two beautiful boys? What is the matter with you?"

Michael walked to the fridge and took out two bottles of water. He passed one to Benita and sat on the edge of his desk. "Benita, you are a young, beautiful, skinny, hot woman. I'll bet your husband loves showing you off. It's not so much being white; it's the fact you take care of yourself. Men don't like it when their wives give birth and think they have earned the right to let themselves go. Men are visual creatures. We think about sex fifty to seventy-five times a day. It's hard to get excited about an overweight black woman. I don't want to go outside the marriage, but what choice do I have? I am not going to wrestle with a fat woman every night."

Benita smiled and opened her bottle of water. She slowly took a sip, put the lid back on the bottle and said, "Michael, your wife may not be excited about the sloppy job you have been doing in the bedroom, but love hides a multitude of faults. Is her race a factor in this? Did the two of you discuss having children before you had them?"

"Yes, but we never discussed gaining all that weight. Don't be crazy, Benita. I married a black woman and I do not apologize for it. Race is not an issue for me. But my friends sometimes stumble over it."

"Michael, you are a selfish man. What if you were the one who had the babies? Would you like it if she treated you like an outdated incubator? Women are self-sacrificing beings. We don't generally weigh the option of weight gain over bearing children. We loan our bodies for nine months for children. We go through morning sickness, hormonal imbalance, sore breasts, and so much more. Our spines move back as far as they can go. Our pelvic bones between our legs come apart. These cute little breasts ache with the pain of anticipation of childbirth. Did I say that already? Everything in a woman's body goes through painful changes, before and after we give birth. And after all of that , we have to deal with some ungraceful, unthankful, unholy, self-righteous, peer-pressure-challenging fools like you. How could you be so uncaring, Michael? It's okay to say to her in a loving way, you would like her to lose the weight, but you have taken this to a whole other level."

"I don't have to sit here and be lectured by you who have never had a child. Get out before I throw you out."

Benita sat up, uncrossed her legs, and reached for her makeup compact to replace her red lipstick. "Michael, if you keep talking to me in such a disrespect tone I am going to treat you like a hostile enemy. And before you say anything, do not let this skinny, pretty face fool you. Now that was my nice version. Do you want to meet Attorney Porter or do you want to continue dealing with Benita as a friend of the family? I can guarantee Attorney Porter has connections all the way to the FBI and all she has to do is make a phone call, give them a name and an address, and your life becomes a living hell in a matter of minutes. Now—" Benita stood up. "—do you think your male ego is enough to deal with the Witch Attorney Porter?"

"Benita, I don't want any trouble. I've heard about you. Does Sadie Mae know about you?"

"Sit down, listen, and make sense. What is going on? I know you've had your eyes on the skinny brunette out there at your front desk. You look at her again after today and I will use it against you in divorce court. No more lunch dates and gifts for her. Make today her last day, because you need to focus on your marriage, on the woman who loves you so much she would do anything to save it. If you love her half as much, fix this mess before it gets worse. Do you have any idea what you are doing to her? She is near a nervous breakdown. I've never seen a woman who loved a man as much as she does. Michael, you hurt her and for what?"

Michael sighed. "Look, Benita, I am sorry about what I've put her through, but I have not had a sexual relationship with my receptionist, so I am not firing her."

"I know, Michael, but it was in the making. All you needed was a location, because she was willing. I hope this doesn't turn into a Bill Clinton situation of not knowing when you have had sex. Sadie Mae was a virgin when you married her. I know it took a lot of self-control on both your parts to wait until marriage. You are her one and only love, Michael, and your sons need the two of you. Are you going to throw away six years of marriage for the home wrecker sitting at your front desk?"

"I've been a fool," Michael admitted. "I don't need to fit into the trophy wife club. I want Sadie Mae back. Do you think it is too late to fix this stuff?"

"Michael, Sadie Mae is black," Benita said. "She will always be a black woman, so if the pressure to change her is coming from your new friends then maybe you need to carefully select some friends who accept both of you in the skin you were born with. Go home, Michael. But not until you fire your receptionist and call a temp service and have them send you a middle-aged, married woman."

Michael stood up, walked over, and hugged Benita. "Thank you, Benita, for putting my head back on straight."

"I am glad Benita could help and we did not need to upset Attorney Porter."

Michael laughed. "Attorney Porter sounds like a female Godfather."

"We won't discuss Attorney Porter anymore. Michael, I was born an African American female. I look white. It's the one-fifth black blood in my body that makes me black. I am proud to be black."

"I never knew."

"Most people who look at me cannot tell. My husband is black and

By: Willi Ray

he knows my family. We have nothing to prove to anyone. Yes, we are judged by other people and called ebony and ivory, Jungle Fever, and so many other names. My mother always told me it is not the name people call you, that's as important as the name you answer to. Both my parents are brown-skinned people, but one of them carried the white man DNA gene and it was passed to me. My great-grandmother was white on my father's side and my great-grandmother said the master was in the slave's quarters more than he was in his wife's bed. Therefore, I am the product of both sides. Michael, I am as white as I am black. Look at Mike Jr. He looks like a little white boy, and Keith looks like a mixed child. Black women can give birth to two nations and two different races, all flowing from one blood line.

For the first time, Michael saw the state of devastation he had created by trying to force his wife to change, instead of loving and encouraging her to lose the weight and loving her wherever she was in this season of her life.

"Benita, thank you. To me, my two sons look white, but they are African American, and my wife is black. I think I was thinking if she was slim and beautiful people in my circle would overlook the fact she is a black woman. I realize now somewhere in my sons' lives I have to be able to teach them how to survive as black men in white America. I have to teach them how to survive white racist policemen, how to shun the racially biased world in the skin they are born in. I have not been a realistic about who I am and who my wife is or about the world my sons will grow up in. I used to watch the news and see the white policemen killing black boys and men without cause and I told myself I was grateful my sons were white, but the truth is, my sons are not white, and they are also on the hit list along with the other black men who will be killed at traffic stops. The fear I did not understand as a white man with two white sons has become soul shatteringly clear. One day my boys could be shot because they are black and live in a world that cannot tolerate the sight of black men. How can I teach my two sons about black issues and the fact of why I am married to a black woman? Benita, thank you for opening my eyes, again. How can I thank you more?"

"Go home," said Benita. "Take care of my girl. Dydbie and I came to help Sadie Mae. Now I know you are going to fix things, we will be leaving tomorrow."

Benita took an empty box from Michael's office and walked out to the receptionist's desk. "Honey, today is your last day." While she talked to the receptionist, she was cleaning out her desk. "Your last check will be in the mail. Miss, shut up and listen. This is important."

"Who are you, and why am I being fired?" shouted the receptionist. "Mr. Crenshaw is my boss. You cannot fire me!"

Benita slapped her across the face, grabbed her by her throat. "I told you to shut up and listen. I am not going to tell you again. I hate gutter-snakes slide into these nine-to-five jobs with the idea of sleeping with the boss for promotions. Go snake your way into another man's marriage."

Angry tears ran down the girl's face, as she called for Michael. He refused her outcry.

"Now, here is your box. The elevator is straight ahead. Do not contact Mr. Crenshaw ever again. If you do, I will find you and your life will be over as you know it. Do you hear me?"

"Yes," the girl sputtered.

"Now get out. And remember, you do not sleep with a married man. Understand?"

A shocked look came over the girl's face. She ran to the elevator with her box. Benita pulled her hair back in place. To Michael, she said, "I hope I do not ever have to do this again. Good night, Michael."

Michael stood there with his mouth open.

Benita's phone rang.

"Hello, Benita." Dydbie was crying on the other end of the phone. "Please come to the hospital. It's Sadie Mae. She passed out and hit her head. I tried to reach Michael, but the receptionist kept saying he was in a meeting. I told her it was an emergency, his wife needed him. She said she would let him know when he was out of the meeting."

Benita turned red. "Michael fired her. We will meet you at the hospital."

"What?" Michael asked. "What did she say is wrong with Sadie Mae?"

"She passed out. Dydbie said the doctors are working on her now. Your reception wouldn't let Dydbie talk to you even though she told her your wife needed you. Yes, Michael, you slept with her, but right now my girl needs me."

By: Willi Ray

"I will meet you there." He grabbed his hat and trench coat and locked the door.

Dydbie called again. "Benita, hurry, the doctor said they needed to talk to the next of kin. I called her mother and father. They are on their way."

"Michael is on his way too. Where are the boys?"

"With the neighbor next door."

Sadie Mae's parents, Mr. and Mrs. Franklin, arrived at the hospital. Dr. Brewster came out to meet with them. He told them Sadie Mae's heartbeat was faint. Her blood pressure was in stroke range, and she was in a coma. Mrs. Franklin screamed, "Not my baby!" Her husband held her tight as they continued to listen. He asked if she had been taking any medications. Mrs. Franklin said she had started a new diet and told him the name of the diet.

The doctor did not think the diet had done this to her. "We found a substance in her blood compatible with the Brazilian diet pills," he said. "Was she taking any other medications? Was she suicidal? What was going on in her life that would make her overdose on diet pills?"

Chapter 15.

Michael arrived, and Mr. Franklin told the doctor, "Here is her husband. He wants a skinny wife. Is dead skinny enough?"

The doctor asked Michael if he knew why she would overdose on diet pills. Was she suicidal?

Michael stood there, tears welling up in both eyes. The muscles on the left side of his face nervously jumped. "She is not suicidal. She may have taken more pills than she should have, but not to hurt herself."

"Why was she on a diet?" the doctor asked. "At her height, weighing 140 pounds, she is well within normal weight range. She could carry another twenty pounds and not be overweight. Why was she taking so many pills? Was she under pressure to lose weight?"

"She did lose fifteen pounds," said Michael.

Mr. Franklin walked over and hit Michael in the stomach. "If you had anything to do with this, I will hurt you beyond belief."

Michael said nothing. He was trying to compose himself after having the air knocked out of him. Everyone looked at him as if he had stolen something. He felt so bad. Finally, catching his breath, he asked, "Did she have a stroke?"

"Yes, she had a mild stroke," the doctor answered. "We won't know the damage until she comes out of the coma. We are working to get her blood pressure regulated and to stabilize her. It could be a week or even a month before she comes out of the coma. The brain activity is strong.

Benita asked the doctor, "So Sadie Mae overdosed on diet pills? I don't believe it. The only pills she ever took were her vitamins, and the diet she was on was 1,500 calories. Doctors recommend it to their patients to lose weight safely. I am going to Sadie Mae's house, and I am going to take that house apart looking for whatever she overdosed on."

"Let me do that Benita," Michael said. "I will find it if it is in the house."

He knew he had to find the pills before anyone else and destroy them. He knew the pills were illegal because he had bought them on the black market.

"No," Benita said. "You need to stay here with your wife in case the doctors need to talk to you again. Dydbie and I will go to your house and search everything. I am praying Sadie Mae pulls out of this."

While Mrs. and Mrs. Franklin were on the phone calling people to pray, Michael went to the chapel and broke down. He cried like a baby. The priest was lighting the large white candles. The sound of this man's pain took over the atmosphere in the chapel. He could be heard from one end of the hall to the other. You could hear the pain in his tears and see the hurt on his pale white face, drained of blood. The sound of his crying filled the air ducts and vents in the building. The sound of wailing filled the hospital. People stopped and took notice of the deep, sorrowful screams coming from the chapel. The place of peaceful solitude was filled with grief. It was a sound even heaven had to stop and pay attention to. There was a powerful hurt lent itself to a troubled man's tears. The guilt for pushing Sadie Mae so hard to lose the weight was now eating him alive.

Between tears, Michael confessed to the priest, "If only I knew she was ready to die to please my selfish request."

He prayed with deep sorrow. "Lord, please don't let her die. Please forgive me for my stupidity. I am so sorry. Lord, if you wake her up, in her right mind, I promise to be a good husband and father. God, I have not prayed in a long time. I don't know the right words to say. Please, save my wife."

He pulled on the priest's clothing. "Please, you know God well. He listens to you. Please tell him I am so sorry. Tell him I am a good person. I did not mean to hurt my wife."

He cried some more. "Priest, said a prayer for her. Call her name. It's Sadie Mae. If you don't say anything else, call her name before the Throne of Grace. Say it! Say it! Call it! Say a prayer for Sadie Mae."

The priest rubbed Michael's back and called out Sadie Mae's name. After ten minutes of praying, Michael thanked the priest, composed his self and wiped his eyes and went back to Sadie Mae's room. He sat beside her bed and stroked her short black curly hair. The room was filled with many beeping sounds of hell. Everything seemed to be too loud and added to Michael's stress. He was barely breathing and his heart was filled with the self-inflicted

By: Willi Ray

pain of a broken heart. He was filled with so many regrets and the thoughts of yesterday filled his mind.

"Our boys need you, Sadie Mae," he whispered. "Please come back to me, to us. I never realized you are my world. I don't exist without you. Your eyes are beautiful even when they are closed. I love your rich brown skin and I miss your beautiful full lips."

He sobbed for a few minutes, started again. "Sadie Mae, I don't know if you can hear me or not, but I have to say I am so sorry. I can't believe I did this to you. I did not mean to hurt you. I was trying to fit into the trophy wives society, a group of young professional men exploiting their wives."

He cried aloud and prayed between tears, begging God for mercy.

Gradually, the room seemed to transform as it faded into a white cloud of silky mist. His eyes were so filled with tears he could not make out the image sitting in the big white throne slowly came into view. The floor looked as if it were made of priceless gold. The throne sat in mid-air, suspended by a rainbow of purple, yellow, and red flashes of bright light. The rainbow was suspended in air on nothing.

It seemed there were millions of winged creatures filling the area, saying, "Worthy is the Lamb that was slain." Another one said, "Glory to the King of Kings. Praise the Holy Lamb of God." There was a soothing sound of music caused a calming of the soul. The music was alive. It moved and surrounded the throne, and like butterflies, it flew through the heavens. There was a river flowing in the air and the water sparkled with crystal diamonds. The robe worn by the man on the throne was the whitest white ever known to man.

Human eyes could not behold and focus long on the image. The glow radiating from the bronze-colored man seemed to change shades every split-second. On his feet were sandals made of air with rubies and other precious stones. His voice echoed a thousand thunderous sounds commanded obeisance.

Michael dropped to his knees when he realized he was no longer on earth, but possibly having an out-of-body experience. "Who are you, my Lord?" he asked. "Are you here for punishment for what I did to my wife? Lord, have mercy! Have mercy on us! Please forgive me and take my life, but spare her life, I pray."

"Your prayers have been heard," the thunderous voice uttered. And like that, Michael was back in the hospital. The irritating sounds of the heart monitor snapped him back to reality.

Still crying, he kissed Sadie Mae's forehead. "Sadie Mae, the boys need you. And so, do I. We can't live without you." He leaned in to kiss her lips. "I need you, Sadie Mae."

When Benita returned to the hospital, she found Michael pacing outside Sadie Mae's room. "I did not find anything," she told him. "How is Sadie Mae?"

"She is not responding," Michael said. "I am afraid she is going to slip away from us. I am afraid God may take her from me because I didn't appreciate her."

"Michael, you have to keep talking to her," Benita said. "She can still hear you. When she is stronger, she will come back to us."

Two weeks later, Michael was still spending nights at the hospital. He whispered to his wife, "Mike Jr. sent you a get-well letter. Dydbie and your parents are taking care of the boys. Keith is missing you so bad. Honey, I have never thanked you for giving me those two beautiful boys. Benita explained in detail the trauma the female body goes through in order to give birth to a child. I have been so selfish, mostly because I can't give birth and did not understand the sacrifice and the gift you women are to men. I love you. Please don't leave us, Sadie Mae. We need you. Please wake up."

Fresh tears flowed. There was no earthly sound in the room besides the beeping of the machines. But heaven heard every word. His hot, salty tears fell on her face, on her eyes and onto her lips. After many of his tears filled the cradle of her eyes, they ran down her cheeks and into her ears. The tears from the overflowing of her ears ran down to the bleached white sheets. He looked down and noticed how wet Sadie Mae's face was, and he wiped her face and laid his head on her chest and whispered, "Come back to me."

Sadie Mae squeezed his finger. Michael jumped up. He pushed the call button and screamed out to the nurse, "She is awake! Help! Come quick!"

By: Willi Ray

The nurse came into the room. Sadie Mae was still in the coma, but there was more brain activity. The nurse checked her vital signs. Her blood pressure was back to normal, and she had rapid eye movement. Another nurse changed the IV bag and fussed over Sadie Mae, but she did not come out of the coma.

Michael stood there looking over the nurse's shoulder, anticipating Sadie Mae opening her eyes. The three nurses blocked his view, but he kept moving from side to side to see while repeating the words, "Sadie Mae, wake up. I love you, Sadie Mae." he pushed his way between the nurses and lifted her hand to his lips. "Speak to me, Baby," he whispered.

The nurses asked him to leave while they cared for Sadie Mae. "It may have been involuntary muscle movement," they told him. "It happens when a patient has been in a coma for a while. Please, let us take care of your wife. We will let you know when to come back in."

"She is going to wake up any minute," Michael said. "I want to be here when she opens her eyes."

"We will come get you, Sir, if she wakes up." The nurse led him to the door and closed it.

Michael watched through the small glass insert in the door. He saw her foot move. He was sure of it. He ran back into the room, calling her name.

The nurse asked him again to leave.

"Sadie Mae, I need you," Michael yelled as they tried to escort him out.

"Michael? Where are my babies?" Sadie Mae's lips moved slowly.

Michael pushed the nurses out of the way and stroked his wife's face. Her eyes opened slowly. Michael never thought he could be so happy to see those lovely dark brown eyes. Sadie Mae," he whispered. "I thought I might never hear the sound of your voice again. Sadie Mae, I am so sorry for how I have treated you. Please forgive me."

The nurse gave Sadie Mae some water. Her hand reached up to touch the white bandage on her forehead. She started to pull at it. The nurse moved her hand away several times. "You have stitches, honey. The bandage has to stay on."

BROKEN

"What happened to me?" Sadie Mae asked. "Why am I in the hospital?"

"You overdosed on some diet pills," Michael told her.

"I was not taking any diet pills," Sadie Mae whispered, confused.

Now she was awake, Michael was not ready to tell her what he had done. "How many vitamins did you take?" Michael asked.

Sadie Mae asked, "Michael, where are my babies? I want to see my babies."

"They will come see you later. Baby, how many vitamins did you take?"

"I don't know, maybe five or six in two days. I was not feeling well, so I thought the vitamins would fight off the virus or cold I was catching. Where are my boys?

"You took three a day?"

"Yes, Michael, why? I've been taking One-A-Day vitamins for seventeen years and I have never gotten sick from them."

"Sir, you need to let her rest," the nurse said.

"Alright. I will go get the boys," Michael said. "I love you, Baby." He kissed her cheek. "I will be back in thirty minutes."

Sadie Mae's parents came into the room. Her mother cried and thanked God for waking up her baby. Benita, Lyn, and Dydbie came in later, and they all hugged Sadie Mae and said, "Welcome back."

"We missed you," Benita added. She asked, "Hey, girl, what did you take?"

Lyneil asked, "Where are those diet pills you were taking? We all looked for those diet pills, but we could not find them."

Sadie Mae was getting irritated. "Stop with the diet pills. I am not taking any diet pills. Why do you all think I took some diet pills? As bad as things got with Michael, I still have two boys to live for. I am not suicidal. I am not going to die over no man, husband or not. I love Michael, but I will not die for him."

By: Willi Ray

The nurse came into the room. "Ladies, we need to let the patient rest now. Her vitals are rising, so make it short, so she can rest. You all can come back in a couple of hours."

"Nurse, we will leave in a minute," Benita said. "Sadie Mae, don't get upset. We are concerned about how you got here. Something doesn't add up. How did you overdose on diet pills without any knowledge to taking the pills? We searched your house from top to bottom, and we found nothing."

Lyneil said, "Hey, Benita, I am sorry, but I almost forgot about the vitamins I found—a bottle of One-A-Day. They didn't smell like vitamins to me."

"May I have the bottle?" Benita asked. "I will take it to the doctor, so he can check to see if this is what he is looking for. It is not a diet pill, but maybe it has the same ingredients as the diet pills." Benita took the lid off the bottle and smelled the pills; she took them to the nurses' station. "The doctor needs to test these pills for whatever Sadie Mae overdosed on."

When she returned, Sadie Mae asked, "Are you thinking my One-A-Day vitamins made me sick? No way."

Michael made it to the parking lot, got into the car, and put his key into the lock. Was all this his fault? Had he almost killed his wife, trying to force her to fit into his ideal of a size-four dream woman? Why couldn't he love her and let her be? He had tried to make her into the carbon image of the ladies in the magazines. He hadn't realized most of those ladies paid a high price to look a certain way. A woman had to establish a neutral zone between being herself and being the woman, her husband wanted her to be. Why wasn't her love enough? He had to get those vitamins before anyone else found them.

He pushed his red Corvette as fast as he could to get home to retrieve those pills before anyone else did. He whipped into the garage and got out of his car. He waved at the neighbors as he entered the house through the garage. He went straight into the bathroom. Where was that bottle of vitamins? Sadie Mae must have taken them to work with her. He had to keep the bottle out of the wrong hands.

The man he bought them from lied, he said they were safe. But he almost killed his wife. He could go to jail for attempted murder. How could he have been so ignorant? He went into the bedroom and went through all the drawers and everywhere he thought Sadie Mae might hide a small bottle. He couldn't find anything.

He sat down on the bed for a while, his head in his hands. God, if you will help me out of this I promise to be a better person and a better husband, he prayed. He walked out of the bedroom into the kitchen and looked through every drawer and cabinet.

He promised Sadie Mae he would bring the boys to see her. He walked over to the neighbor's house. Miss Walker was a widow, her gray hair pulled up into a bun. He blew his nose and wiped his eyes rang the doorbell.

Miss Walker looked over her glasses, trying to read him before asking questions. "How is that pretty wife of yours?"

Michael was shaking, knowing Sadie Mae was in the hospital, and he put her there. He cleared his throat. "She is getting better. She has a virus."

"Yes, she does have a virus," Miss Walker began, "and it is called you, Michael. I've seen the way you treat your wife. Son, you should be a shame of yourself. You have a good wife. She is smart, and pretty, too. Have you seen how good she is with your sons?"

Michael sighed. "Miss Walker, where are my boys? I have to get back to the hospital."

Miss Walker retreated down the hall, still fussing about Michael's failures, and returned with the boys. Michael put the boys into the car and answered their questions about their mom. "She is okay right now, and she is asking for you two."

Dr. Cain walked into Sadie Mae's room. "Sadie Mae, can we talk in private? I have some information about the diet pills."

Sadie Mae said, "You can talk in front of these ladies. They are dear friends. This is my mom and my dad, Mr. and Mrs. Franklin."

"How are you folks doing?" Dr. Cain shook everyone's hands. "Now I am going to make this simple. Sadie Mae, these are not vitamins in this bottle. These pills are Brazilian diet pills. They were outlawed by the American Food and Drug Administration. These are sold only on the black market. Where did

By: Willi Ray

you get these?"

"What? Black market?" Sadie Mae was confused. "I bought those vitamins at Walgreen two months ago. So why am I now getting sick? I have taken those pills for sixty days and have not gotten sick."

Mrs. Franklin took a hold of Sadie Mae's hand. "Honey, these are not vitamins. These are illegal pills purchased on the black market. Tell us, how did you get them?"

Mr. Franklin shook his head in disbelief.

Chapter 16

"No, Dad," Sadie Mae said. "Do not go there. My own husband would not stoop to a new low. Momma, Michael would not do this to me." Her tears told everyone in the room she did not believe what she was saying.

"These pills cannot be consumed for a long period on time," the doctor continued. "You had a dangerous reaction to these pills. The question remains, how did you get them, and why are they in your vitamin bottle?"

"I don't know," said Sadie Mae.

Benita asked the doctor if she could have the bottle back.

The doctor looked at Benita. "This is either attempted homicide or attempted suicide. Either way, I have to report this to the DEA."

"What is going on?" Lyneil asked. "It sounds like someone put those pills in that bottle."

Dydbie said, "Sadie Mae, I hope this is not as bad as it sounds. DEA?"

"This has Michael written all over it," Benita said. "Attempted murder is serious. I am your attorney. Attorney Porter is now on the case."

"Michael would not do this," Sadie Mae asserted. "He has his faults, but not hurting me."

Lyneil said, "Sadie Mae, he wasn't trying to hurt you. He was trying to force you to lose the weight and almost killed you."

Sadie Mae started to cry. "All of you, leave. I want to be alone."

Mrs. Franklin stood, but she stayed and held Sadie Mae's hand and stroked her hair while she cried. The nurse came in and gave her a sedative, so she could rest.

Sadie Mae knew Michael was the only one who had access to the house and also had the motive to put those diet pills in the vitamin bottle. She cried because it hurt to think he would go this far.

Benita was hot as hell. "Where is Mr. Crenshaw?" She paced in the waiting room like a caged lion. The doctor picked up the phone to call the police to report a crime of poisoning. She asked him to wait until Michael got back to the hospital.

Soon Michael arrived with the boys. Benita caught him as they entered Sadie Mae's room. "I need to speak to you alone," she said.

Mike Jr. whispered, "Mom, you are awake. I talked to God and asked him to wake you up. Mom, you have been asleep for a long time. Are you going to stay asleep now? I miss you, Mom."

Sadie Mae said, "I miss you too, my sweet boy. Come and give me a big hug." She barely opened her eyes.

"Mommy, you sleep too much," Keith said. "Why can't you sleep in your own bed? Did I make too much noise for you to sleep at home? I am staying here with you, Mom." He climbed into the bed and lay on his mom.

"Come on in, sweetie." She beckoned to Mike Jr. "I love you two. Keith, I see you are wearing your Michael Jackson gloves."

"Mommy, I am Michael Jackson's biggest fan," Keith said. "He is cool! I am going to sing and dance like Michael Jackson when you get home."

Michael and Benita walked down the hall to talk. Michael was busy telling Benita about his love for his family. He said, "I never dreamed I would be in this situation."

She looked around to see the positioning of the cameras and mirrors with the security system. Michael was still talking and following Benita so closely he had not noticed she moved out of range of the security cameras and security guards. She hit Michael so hard he fell backward. "I told you I would kill you if you ever hurt my girl." She straddled him, she took her gun out of her pocket and put it in his mouth. "If you lie to me I will pull this trigger and send you to hell with all the skinny people. Now Michael, we found a vitamin bottle with diet pills in it. This is the reason Sadie Mae is in this hospital. Please make me understand why you did this to your wife."

Michael twitched, and she jammed the gun a little deeper into his mouth. "I can prosecute you for attempted murder, so make it good, and maybe I won't kill you. Now listen to me, Michael, I am going to remove this gun from your mouth and place it in your left ear. Don't give me a reason to shoot you. Now talk."

Looking dazed, Michael could not make eye contact with Benita. "I am so sorry, Benita. I did do this, and I cannot justify my actions."

"It's not Benita. This is Attorney Porter. Now give me one good reason not to shoot you. Talk!"

"Please, Benita—Sorry, I mean Attorney Porter—you got to believe I had no idea this would ever happen in a million years. I thought I could force her to lose the weight, and she would be happy to get the weight off."

Benita slapped the crap out of him. "So, you were willing to kill her to get the weight off."

Michael groaned. "I was trying to fit into a social group at that time in my life. I thought it was a status move to fit into the upper crust of the American elite. I felt as if I deserved to be a member of the trophy wives' group. I felt Sadie Mae's weight was blocking me from getting into this elite class. I am so sorry. Words cannot express my sorrow and shame of what I've done. This is not a crime of hate. It is a grown man falling under peer pressure, trying to keep up with the Jones's, Attorney Porter."

Benita stood up and helped Michael up. She kneed him in the balls, and he fell back down. "I want you to remember this, stupid white man. If Sadie Mae dies, you and your parents will die as well. Now, you have to tell Sadie Mae and her family what you have done and hope she doesn't press changes."

"I saw the police on my way in," Michael said. "Are they here for me?"

Benita said nothing. She adjusted her clothes and checked her makeup.

"I don't deserve Sadie Mae," Michael said. "If she decides not to forgive me and press charges, I will understand."

"I don't think you truly understand," Benita snarled.

Michael walked into Sadie Mae's room and asked Dydbie to take the boys to get some ice cream. Dydbie and Lyneil started to walk out with the boys. As she walked by Michael, Lyneil hissed, "Stupid man syndrome! Stupid! Stupid! Someone needs to beat the hell out of you. Mr. Franklin must have hit you in the face to teach you some sense. I hope he comes back and finishes the job." This was followed by a string of rapid Italian words.

"I made a mistake," Michael whispered. "I did not mean to hurt her."

"Eat dirt and die!" Lyneil replied.

Dydbie sneered, "Bring it down a notch, Lyn. He is not worth getting all worked up over. Michael, do we need to get the police to come pat you down to make sure you do not put anything in her IV to make her lose weight?"

Michael sat down on Sadie Mae's bed. "Honey, I need to tell you something."

Benita walked in with Mr. and Mrs. Franklin.

Sadie Mae said, "Where were the two of you? What were you and Dydbie talking about?"

"Baby, let me talk right now," Michael replied. "This is important."

"Michael, what is going on? Where is Benita? I need her."

Benita said, "I am here. Listen to Michael right now."

"I'll let you talk to Benita later," Michael said, "but right now, Sadie Mae, I need to tell you something."

"Okay. Michael, you are scaring me. What's wrong?"

Michael stood up, sat down again. "Sadie Mae, sweet, sweet, Sadie Mae, you know how I've been trying to get you to lose weight and all the fighting about the weight gain."

"Come here, honey," Sadie Mae said. She took his hand.

Michael's voice started cracking before the first tear of repentance fell. "I bought some diet pills on the black market and put them in your vitamin bottle."

"You did what?"

Furious, Sadie Mae's father stormed out of the room and her mother followed, in tears.

"Mom, Dad, come back please," Sadie Mae said.

Michael took her hand. "Sadie Mae, I had a moment of insanity. I did not know those pills could have killed you. I am so sorry. I was so busy trying to fit into a world that asked me to choose image and perception over the love of a good woman. Honey, I am so sorry. I am so sorry! Please forgive me."

"Get out, you fool! Get out!" Sadie Mae screamed. "You could have killed me. What would you have done if they wanted you to bleach me as white as you are? Get out! Get out!"

The shock was too much for her fragile state of health. She started pushing the call button.

"Get out, Michael," Benita added. "If she dies, I will be pressing charges."

Nurses came running to the code blue. Sadie Mae's heartbeat was off the monitor. It was beeping double beats. Her blood pressure was rising quickly. She kept right on screaming and crying. "I loved you, and you tried to kill me." She tried to get out of bed. "Let me at him! I will break his neck," she screamed.

Five nurses were busy holding her down and flushing medicine into the IV line. Soon her words started to slur and her body became lifeless.

The doctor tried to put Michael out the room, but he would not leave. He was a nervous wreck. He froze in his tracks seeing Sadie Mae was operating on sheer emotion, sheer pain, and disappointment in him. He didn't notice the two policemen at the nurses' desk asking for the doctor.

Thoughts went through Michael's mind of how he was supposed to protect and keep her safe, but to fit into another man's idea of happiness, he sold his soul. The worst thing about it all was he didn't know why it seemed so important to him at the time, and now it was a painful memory.

The nurses saw he was in a state of shock. Fear gripped his body as he watched Sadie Mae slip away into a coma again, this time right before his eyes. He was helpless, but not without blame this time. A mixture of emotions ran rapidly through his soul. A plethora of nurses and doctors were working furiously to stabilize her vitals. She stopped moving and fighting. The screaming faded into the background. A painful silence filled the room.

The bitter chill made his ears pop as the loudest sound of silence he had ever heard filled the air. This silent was so loud it blew his world to pieces. The thunderous sound of silence drowned out the pounding of his heartbeat in his ears.

Sadie Mae lay still. There were so many hands moving in the room he could not see Sadie Mae anymore. Michael was in a state of shock, his mouth frozen open. Benita started crying.

Dydbie came running as more nurses responded to the code blue. Mrs. Franklin dropped her purse and started running down the hall toward her daughter's room, calling on the name of Jesus. Mr. Franklin took the boys to the play room, guided by two nurses taking their break there. He asked one nurse to help him with the boys and the other to see what was going on.

Benita came out of the room crying. She slapped her hand against the tile wall in the hall. She called her husband and asked him to come.

The doctor told Sadie Mae's mother she stopped breathing three times and now she was in a second coma. The doctor told Mrs. Franklin he had never seen this kind of nightmare in all of his 30 years as a doctor. We are still trying to stabilize her blood pressure, and her heartbeat is weak. "We will watch and monitor her throughout the night," he told her.

Mrs. Franklin asked what had caused the set back.

The doctor looked into Michael's face. Michael's eyes were glazed with fear. "Her husband did this," he replied. "Senseless, why couldn't he have waited until she was stronger to give her such bad news?"

When Mr. Franklin heard what the doctor said, he stormed into Sadie Mae's room. "Where is he? I am sick and tired of him acting a fool with my little girl."

"Please, Mr. Franklin," the doctor said, "save energy for your daughter. She needs both of you now. She is in critical condition."

Michael slowly walked into the hall and fainted. Lyneil kept on walking past Michael's lifeless body on the hall floor as a pack of nurses rushed to his aid. He was admitted to the hospital, and the nurses put him in a bed next door to Sadie Mae's room. He lay there in a state of shock.

The next thing he knew, he was surrounded by the walls of silence and the piercing morning sun shining on his face. It was morning, and he felt as if he had passed through twenty-four midnights. He hurt so bad inside. He wished for death, but death fled from him in shame. His punishment now would be living, knowing he nearly killed the woman he loved, not once, but twice. He tried to get up but his legs were wobbly, and he shook all over. He

By: Willi Ray

kept pushing himself from the bed. His one thought was to see Sadie Mae. He had to know if she was okay.

The nurses tried to keep him in the bed, but he came back into Sadie Mae's room. She lay there, unconscious. Michael looked at all the machines hooked up to her. "What have I done?" he whispered.

"Sir, you should not be in here," the nurse said. "The doctor said to keep you out because you are upsetting the patient."

"Is she in another coma?"

"Yes, she is. Her heart has sustained harsh damage." Michael went back to his room when the nurse threatened to call security. Nothing seemed real anymore, he kept trying to wake up but never escaping his eternal hell.

Benita brought some white roses and Sadie Mae's favorite song by Anita Baker. "What's wrong?" Benita asked as she sat beside the bed and talked to Sadie Mae and let the song play. "It's safe to come out now, Sadie Mae. I promise to protect you. I won't let anyone hurt you. What's wrong? What's wrong with you, Sadie Mae? What's wrong? Talk to me. You know all your girls are here to see you. Talk to us. We love you."

In his room next door, Michael heard Anita Baker singing, and he remembered Sadie Mae singing "Sweet Love" to him on their wedding day. He prayed again. "Dear Lord, it's me again. First, I want to thank you for the blessing of bringing my wife out of the coma the first time. I need you again, Lord. Can you please wake her up again? I need her to be alright. Her boys and her husband need her right now. I know I am the reason she is in that coma, but I need to ask, can you spare one more miracle? Lord, if you give me back my wife and my marriage I will give you my heart and soul. Lord, I am asking a life for a life. God, in case someone needs to be a ransom for Sadie Mae's life, please take mines and let her live. She has two boys and they need her. I have learned love hides a multitude of faults."

He squeezed his hands together and closed his eyes. "Whatever her shortcomings were, Lord, they should have been covered by my love for her. Lord, I know sometimes we are so busy looking at what we do not have we forget to be thankful for what we do have. I am so thankful for having known Sadie Mae and for the family she gave me, for the unconditional love she gave me. Everything I am today is because she loved me. Lord, you said if I have faith the size of a mustard seed I could move mountains. You said to ask and it shall be given, seek and I shall find, knock and the door shall be opened. I am knocking, seeking, and asking. Give Sadie Mae back her health and strength and teach her how, to one day forgive me. Lord, it is Christmas Eve. This is the season for miracles, and I am looking for a miracle."

Michael got up when the nurse brought in his release papers. He went to get the boys from his mother-in-law. It was snowing, and the wet flakes covered the windshield faster than the wipers could remove them. He turned into the subdivision. There a father and sons were building a snowman. The tire tracks ran deep in the snow led to his in-law's house. The sky around the housetops was filled with smoke from the chimneys. Icicles formed inches long from the roofs. It looked as if the earth was washing away her sins and his as well. The wind-chill factor was below zero and dropping fast. It was a Chicago type of winter—bone cold.

He was so engrossed in his thoughts he did not notice all the things happening around him. His one thought was getting his boys and getting back to the hospital. Michael did not see the police car behind him when he turned into the subdivision until he heard the siren. The policeman walked to Michael's car. "Sir, were you aware you were driving sixty miles an hour in a residential area?"

"Sir, my wife is in the hospital. I am so sorry for speeding, explained Michael"

The policeman looked at Michael's license. "Michael Crenshaw, you are a suspect in an attempted homicide. Step out of the car."

"Sir, I did not hit anyone. Why am I being arrested?"

"You have to come downtown for questioning. Your rights will be read to you. Place your hands behind your head." The policeman cuffed him and put him in the patrol car. The police explained to Michael he was being arrested for attempted murder of his wife.

"I did not mean to hurt her," Michael cried.

At the police station, after being questioned and fingerprinted, he was allowed one phone call. He sat there thinking who he should call. He called Benita.

"Benita, don't hang up, I need an attorney. Please help me. I need to be at the hospital with Sadie Mae."

"I cannot represent you, Michael, because I will be Sadie Mae's lawyer if she wants to press charges. But for the children's sake, I will bail you out because they need you now."

Benita did not want Mike and Keith to be without both parents for Christmas. She posted Michael's bail and drove him to his car. "Michael, finish whatever you need to do. Get the boys and get back to the hospital. At least we can all spend Christmas together. Raheem is here and I need to pick him up from the airport."

Michael did not look at Benita when she dropped him off at his car. Benita grabbed his hand. "Michael, I am asking you to forgive me if I hurt you, but I will fight for all three of those ladies. We have a sisterhood bond beyond your understanding. Michael nodded his head, but didn't say a word. I am praying for a Christmas miracle, said Benita."

When Michael arrived at his in-law's house to collect his sons, Mr. Franklin answered the door. Michael was feeling so low it took everything he had to keep going. There has to be a light at the end of this dark, horrible pit of hell.

Michael forced himself to make eye contact. "Sir, can I talk to you?"

"Son, I got a good mind to beat you like you stole the Good Lord's Supper for what you did to my baby. I will beat some sense into you. Son, you don't have the sense God gave a skunk, a stripe down his back and a belly full of funk. I am a Christian, and it is taking all I have not to choke the life out of you. What do you need to talk about, man? Have you told your parents about the evil you did to your wife?" Now, you want to talk to me. You could not talk to me before you tried to kill my daughter, but now you want to talk. Talk about what, white boy?

"Sir, I understand your anger. I did not mean to hurt her and I want to apologize to the both of you. I did a dumb thing. Sometimes a man can do something so dumb; he is ashamed to explain why he did it. This is one of those things. Sir, if you want to beat me down, I do understand, I deserve it. I was willfully selfish and that's what got me into this situation. Words cannot express my sorrow right now. All I can do is ask for forgiveness, sir." "You want me to forgive you. What? I am not God, step back man, I am fresh out of forgiveness, yelled Mr. Franklin."

Michael stretched out his hand to shake Mr. Franklin's hand. Sir please, Michael begged. Mr. Franklin refused; with a quick flick of his wrist he slapped Michael breathless.

"Be a man; look me in my eyes if you want my forgiveness. That is the problem with some men; they cannot justify their male ego narcissism to their wives' father. They forget the woman they married still has a family who loves her. When you hurt her, you hurt her mother and father." I should kill you for what you did but I'll let the law deal with you. His voice got louder as anger and hurt took control of him. "What kind of man poisons his wife to make her lose weight? You want her dead, Michael? You want her dead? Dead people don't gain weight, Michael."

Mrs. Franklin heard the heated words and quickly joined her husband. "Son, we forgive you," she said, "but we are still upset with you right now. I got the boys' things in this bag by the door. All your Christmas gifts are in the big bag. We will pray for you and Sadie Mae. You go on now, go on. We got to get to the hospital too."

Michael hugged Mrs. Franklin, his tears dripped down her neck. He dried his eyes and took Keith into his arms and held them close. Mike Jr. walked beside him to the car. When Michael set little Keith down, he ran into the yard and made a snowball and hit his daddy in the head. "You hurt Mommy," he shouted. "He threw another one and another one. Michael chocked back his pain, took hold of his son and kissed him and placed him in the Batman car seat. "It was an accident, Honey. I am so sorry. I did not mean to hurt Mommy." Michael Jr. never opened his mouth. He got into the front seat and locked the door.

"Boys, we need to go buy Mommy a Christmas gift," he said.

Mike's face lit up. "I know what Mom wants. She wants a watch with diamonds on it."

"No," Keith corrected, "Mommy wants a puppy named Ben. Like Michael Jackson's rat, Ben."

"Keith, you want a puppy, not Mom," Michael said.

By: Willi Ray

"Mommy will be upset with us if we do not get her a puppy, Daddy, please, don't disappoint her on Christmas."

"Keith, what kind of puppy does she want?"

"A brown dog name Ben with big ears. His name is Ben."

"Okay, let's go find Ben. Mike Jr., you can pick out the diamond watch."

"Yes. What are you going to get her, Daddy?"

"I've been talking to God about it."

While the boys were playing with the puppies, Michael walked a few steps away to telepathically talk to Sadie Mae. "Sadie Mae, we are and have been soul mates, so I know you can hear me wherever I am. You have always been able to feel my emotions. I need you to feel and listen to me. I need you to wake up, Honey. Tomorrow is Christmas, and the best gift you could give me is you. Wake up. Come back to me. Sadie Mae, Sadie Mae, Sadie Mae. Remember the first time I told you I loved you? I know you remember. Remember when and how I purposed to you? At our graduation party the DJ asked you to sing Anita Baker's "Angel." When you hit the last note, I fell on my knees and begged you to marry me. You are all I ever thought about, my dark and lovely angel. Sadie Mae, I still love you like crazy. I love you enough until if you want to press charges when you wake up I will gladly go to jail. I made a deal with God, a life for a life. And if there needs to be a ransom to bring you back, I will give up my life if it means you would be given back your health and strength."

"I found Ben, Daddy!" Keith came running. "He is the puppy with the big white ears. Daddy, come on and see Ben."

Michael looked at the puppies, it was a brown cocker spaniel. Keith kept calling him Ben as if the dog knew his name. "Yes, we will buy Ben."

"Michael Jackson had a rat named Ben and I have a puppy named Ben," Keith bubbled.

"I thought the puppy was for Mom," Mike Jr. corrected.

"Mommy can play with him too."

"Okay," Michael said, "now let's go get the watch. I have to go to the hospital to check on Mom."

"Daddy, is Mom coming home for Christmas?" Mike asked.

"Very soon," Michael said.

Michael took the boys home and made dinner for them. Mike Jr. asked, "Daddy, did you hurt Mom? I heard people whispering you hurt Mom."

"Son, I did hurt Mom. But it was not my intention to hurt her. I did something stupid. I wish I could take it back, but I can't, son."

"I am old enough to understand, Dad. What did you do to my mommy?"

"Mike, you are six years old, and it is hard to explain."

"Dad tell me. What did you do?"

"Son, eat, and we can talk about it later."

Mike started screaming. "Now, Daddy. Tell me now! I am not a baby. Tell me now. I am not hungry anyway. What is wrong with Mom?"

Michael sighed. "Mike, I gave Mom some diet pills that made her sick."

"Did you know they would make her sick, Dad?"

"No, son. I thought I was helping her. I am so sorry. I was selfish and only thinking about myself. You know how I tell you about peer pressure and how people from certain clubs and groups try to make you follow some stupid rules to be a part of their group or club? Well, I have some friends who have an elite group, and they won't let me in unless your mother and I fit the profile. So, I tried to change Mom to fit in with this group of people. I wanted them to like me and accept me, which was wrong. I did not make the right decision for me and your mom. I should have walked away. Those are unhappy people who are not happy unless they make other people feel bad. I now realize I have everything I need to be happy and I love your mother the way she is. So, son, I am sorry, and I apologize to you and your brother for what I did to Mom."

"Dad, can you fix Mom back like she was? Dad, Mom loves you so she will forgive you." He started to cry. "Fix her, Dad, please. I want Mom back at home with us."

Keith started to cry as well, "Daddy, did you learn a lesson on peer pressure? Mom said we should think for ourselves and be the better person. Daddy, bring Mommy home, please. I miss Mommy. I can't wait for her to meet Ben."

Michael said, "Listen, boys, this problem is bigger than I. So, I have been talking to God and asking for his help. Put your coats on. I need to be at the hospital."

He took them over to the neighbor's house while he went to the hospital. He arrived at the hospital at about 6:00pm.

Dydbie was sitting on the left side on the bed talking to Sadie Mae and Lyneil was on the right side, holding her hand. Benita was looking out the window. She saw Michael's image in the glass as he entered the room.

Michael looked at Benita and Dydbie. Both had worried looks on their faces. "How is Sadie Mae?" he asked.

No one answered.

"I hope you don't upset her again," Lyneil finally said.

"Michael, what do you want?" Dydbie asked. "It could be Sadie Mae will still be overweight. You said you can't love a fat woman."

"I said a lot of mean, bad things trying to control Sadie Mae. I know that was wrong and you all have the right to hate me. But I hope you don't, because I need the three of you. Right now, I feel so low there is nowhere to go. I asked God to wake her up tonight. So, I am waiting here until he does."

"Michael, while this is admirable, you are setting yourself up for a great disappointment. Please take it one day at a time. You have no control over when she comes out of the coma. Please keep it together" said Dydbie.

Lyneil added. "The doctor said she shows no signs of coming out of the coma."

"Michael, we know you're stressed out over all this," Dydbie said,

BROKEN

"but Christmas is tomorrow, and the boys need you to be there for them."

Michael stood beside his wife. "Sadie Mae, Baby, I love you, and for you I will do anything. I took the boys shopping and Keith bought you the cutest gift.

Chapter 17

Although I think the little stinker bought it for himself. He is so cute, Sadie Mae. You should see him. Mike Jr., he is getting smarter every day. Honey, he has your smile. He gave me a lecture on peer pressure. He's our son."

Benita, Lyneil, and Dydbie sat around the bed and listened to him talk to Sadie Mae. They realized he loved her and he made a horrible mistake that might cost him his wife.

"Sadie Mae," Michael continued, "Keith is three years old, but he has got Michael Jackson in his blood. He eats all his dinner and goes to his room every day and practices singing Michael Jackson songs, and he dances. I've tried to introduce him to other things and professional people, but he does not show any interest. Sadie Mae, I want to thank you for giving me two wonderful boys. And also, I want to thank you for all your love and support. You are a good wife and I love you so much."

He paused a moment, said, "Sadie Mae, tomorrow is Christmas and the boys are anxious to give you the gifts they picked out for you. Honey, all I want for Christmas is you back in my life. I've been wrong about so many things, so now I want to be a good man for you and a good father for the boys. I heard a wise old man say, 'You never miss the water until the well runs dry.' I know what that means now. I miss you so much, and I took for granted you would always be around." Silent Night by the temptation was on the radio and painted the room with a melancholy chill. For a full 60 seconds everyone was speechless, eyes cloudy with tears and their hearts anticipating a much-needed miracle.

Looking out the window, Benita said, "It is snowing again. I wish Sadie Mae could see this snow. This is one of the reasons she loves Chicago. I don't see much snow where I live. I've always seen this Christmas with snow as magical. It is so beautiful."

The ladies all rushed to the window. The fresh snow made everything look like a beautiful, heavenly place of peace and serenity. Michael stared out the window for a long time. The ladies walked back to their seats. They were beginning to be concerned he stood there at the window so long.

"Michael, come and talk with us," Lyneil said.

Michael stayed at the window. "How can this world be covered with such beauty and glistering white snow and still be filled with heartaches, disappointments, and tears?"

"Michael, come away from the window," Benita said. "Talk to Sadie Mae a little more. I believe she can hear you. The snow is a good sign God heard our prayers. Sadie Mae said Christmas is extra special when it snows. She loves snow. Tell her it is snowing."

Michael walked over to the bed. "Honey, it is snowing. You have to wake up to see this. It is so beautiful. This is God's way of covering the world like he covers our sins with his red blood and makes them white as snow. It is snowing, Sadie Mae."

Sadie Mae moved her fingers.

"Did you see?" Michael exclaimed. He rang for the nurse.

Sadie Mae opened her eyes and looked around the room. She saw Michael and said, "Hello, Honey. I've been with God in heaven. He said I could go back home when it snowed. He told me he loves me so much. He told me to get it out, to cry, and he soothed my heart with his love. He healed my broken heart and gave me a second chance at life." Michael, God he is using this situation to restore your heart and soul. He said he forgives you. Michael, said thank you, Jesus for a second chance.

Lyneil said, "Sadie Mae, I think you were dreaming. God is a spirit."

"Hey there, you ladies," Sadie Mae said. "Good to see you again. One thing I know for myself, God is as real as you and me. Thank you, God for this miracle."

Dydbie said, "Sadie Mae, I missed you. Stay with us this time. Please do not go to sleep again." She kissed her on the cheek.

Mr. and Mrs. Franklin arrived with the boys, they were overjoyed when they saw their daughter awake. They hugged everyone and said, "This is the best Christmas ever."

Michael got slowly down on his knees and whispered, "A life for a life. I will take my family to church. Ladies, I will never be a follower again who buckles under peer pressure. I will be a leader for my family. I promise to love you, Sadie Mae Crenshaw with everything I got. Never again will I chase another man's reality. I have learned happiness is not material things, or the status thing, happiness for me, is Sadie Mae and my boys."

Sadie Mae smiled at everyone. "Michael, I heard every word you said to me. I love you too. Thank you for not giving up on me. Mr. Franklin hugged Michael and said I forgive you son. I can't wait to spend Christmas with my husband, my boys, my mother and father, Raheem, and my three best friends. "I am so proud of how my three best friends represented the support of the sisterhood to the end. You all never left my side. Raheem walked over to Benita and held her tight, then he looked at Michael and gave him the man card nod and smiled as a sign of respect. Sadie Mae joyfully repeated, I heard it's snowing outside. The boys vigorously climbed into Sadie Mae's bed, they kissed her and said Merry Christmas Mommy. The radio perked up again with a happy Christmas song by Donny Hathaway "This Christmas" "This will be a very special Christmas, said Sadie Mae"

THE END

About the Author

Willie Ray aka 'Willi Ray' is a mother of one daughter. She grew up in a family of 10 children where education was the promise to a better life in the search for the American Dream. Being raised by a single parent household there was no money for college so Willi paid her own way through school. She graduated from Webster University with a Bachelor's in Healthcare Administration and an MBA in Business Administration. When asked why she went after an MBA her answer is always "Because they told me I could not have it." Willi is a Revenue Cycle Director of a Hospital. Willi grew up writing plays and songs to entertain the family during family bonding time, this passion gave way to her opening her own Stage Play Theater Production Company, Willi Ray Productions. Her stages plays continue to end with standing ovations and praise for good outstanding performances and well-written plays with life lesson messages. Willi Ray is the author of her mother's life story written at the request of her mother, "A Woman Called Mary." Willi Ray wrote her book "Broken" during a difficult stage in her life of going through a divorce. After a lot of soul searching and emotional struggles of the brokenness of divorce and finding the courage of reevaluating her own self-worth she put pen to paper and gave birth to "Broken, but Not in Despair." Willi's message is with the support of the sisterhood being broken is not the end it is a road of discovery as a woman. It is that time when we find our voice and stand with a renewed hope of strength and self-validation as an all-powerful Woman. This book was written to women about women's issues.

CPSIA information can be obtained
at www.ICGtesting.com
Printed in the USA
LVHW082210170521
687713LV00018B/258